M000119331

Praise for Living with Kids and Dogs... Without Losing Your Mind

"Colleen Pelar has lived it all and she tells it like it is with humor, compassion, and practicality. This book is highly recommended!"

~ JOAN ORR, PHD, Founder of DoggoneSafe.com

"This is one of the best books for families I have read in a long time. I have trained and fostered dogs and thought I was very well read on the subject. And even as someone professionally skilled in animal behavior, socialization, and training, this book really opened my eyes to so many aspects of having dogs in our home. This is a definite must-read for any dog owner or prospective dog owner."

~ NICKY BRADLEY, Families.com

"Many dog-training books are available, and certainly numerous books dispense advice on raising kids, but relatively few address both issues. A professional dog trainer and mother of three, Pelar provides a remedy for the human/dog misunderstandings that can lead to dog bites (or worse), especially those involving children."

~ KAY HOGAN SMITH, Library Journal

"This is a wonderful book. Useful, useful, useful information—all the main points in an extremely easy-to-read style. As a trainer and a mom, Colleen sees the full picture."

~ DR. IAN DUNBAR, Founder of the
Association of Pet Dog Trainers

"Filled with important information about dogs that every parent should know."

~ JODIE LYNN, CEO/Founder of the
Parent to Parent Adding Wisdom Awards

Living with Kids and Dogs
... Without Losing Your Mind:

A Parent's Guide to Controlling the Chaos

Colleen Pelar

Dream Dog Productions, LLC
Woodbridge, VA

Living with Kids and Dogs . . . Without Losing Your Mind:
A Parent's Guide to Controlling the Chaos
By Colleen Pelar

Published by:
Dream Dog Productions, LLC
P.O. Box 4227
Woodbridge VA 22194-4227 USA
www.dreamdogproductions.com

Unattributed quotations are by Colleen Pelar

Pelar, Colleen

Living with kids and dogs . . . without losing your mind: a parent's guide to controlling the chaos/Colleen Pelar

P.cm.

Includes index

ISBN 978-193356212-4

1. Parenting

2. Dogs--Training

Cover by Brier Designs

All photos from Shutterstock.com except p. 40, 111, 112, 113, & 155 (girl in striped dress) from Pam Nashman; p. 35 & 41 from Dream Dog Productions; p. 63, 124, & 162 (yellow labrador) from Colleen Pelar; p. 64 from www.softouchconcepts.com; p. 66 from www. baddogsinc.com; p. 69 from Julie Fudge Smith; p. 76 (logo) from www.familypaws.com; p. 114 from Brigid Ashur; p. 161 (cairn terrier) & 170 from Maureen Daniels.

Cover photo of Sophie the dog by Michael Woodward. Sophie is from Sherry Von Engel, Von Engel Bernese Mountain Dogs, est. 1992, www.vonengelbmds.homestead.com

10   9   8   7   6   5   4   3   2   1

Acknowledgements

New Thoughts for the Second Edition

This second edition is very similar to the first, but with many more photos to help illustrate good and bad interactions between children and dogs. I think photos are a very powerful teaching tool, so I was happy to be able to include more.

One challenge in doing an updated version is that many people have told me that they really like that the book is short. I can talk about dogs for days on end (and often have!), so I worried that I might tip the balance and make the book too long. I tried only to add things that I felt were really necessary and helpful, and I cut a few things here and there to make space.

The years of living with kids and dogs are very challenging, but they go quickly! When the first edition of this book came out, my sons were in junior high and elementary school. Now they tower over me and are preparing for lives on their own. I feel grateful that they were able to share their childhoods with some wonderful dogs and hope that your kids can have the same special gift.

~ Colleen Pelar
November 2012

From the Original Edition

Creating this book has been a long journey. Many people helped along the way.

A big thank you to all the parents and dog trainers who took time to read chapters and give me feedback, including Melissa Alexander, Teoti Anderson, Brigid Ashur, Jennifer Austin, Kris and Randy Busch, Maureen Daniels, Beverly Dernbach, Elizabeth Dernbach, Peter Dernbach, Ian Dunbar (who told me to just start writing, so I did!), Karen Fernan,

Laura Jamar, Susan McCullough (who, when I said someone should write a book about living with kids and dogs, suggested that the right someone might be me), Joyce and Becky Martin, Pat Miller, Leslie Nelson (who coined the term "name game" and often discusses the three keys to success in her lively, informative seminars), Joan Orr, Victoria Schade, Susan Smith, Laura Van Dyne, and Nicole Wilde (for giving me a push right when I needed it and for answering all of my mundane questions). I cannot thank you all enough.

To the most wonderful group of trainers that anyone could work with, the staff of All About Dogs, LLC: Robin Bennett, Keely Bovais, Diana Craig, AnnMarie Dykes, Roz Ferber, Eileen Fulk, Vicki Gotcher, Mary Graham, Chris Johnson, Kim Kirilenko, Pam Nashman, Vicky Shields Harding, Julie Fudge Smith, and Martha Walker. I feel blessed to count you among my friends.

To all the families who have trained with me since 1991, thank you for sharing your dogs and children with me. You inspire me every day.

Most especially, thank you to my own wonderful family. My terrific husband, Jack, has always supported and encouraged my passion for dogs, even though he doesn't share it himself. While I'll never be able to understand how he can resist the incredible charm of dogs, I adore him nonetheless.

My great kids, Justin, Kyle, and Brandon, who helped in so many ways, from supplying names for my imaginary dogs and kids, to posing for hundreds of pictures so I could get just what I wanted, to doing their homework around the various drafts piled upon my desk. Thanks, guys!

Being a mother makes me more sensitive to the needs of all kids. Because of my kids and for yours, I plod on doing my part in the effort to eliminate dog bites to children.

Together, we can help children and dogs live together safely and happily. That is my dream and my passion.

Disclaimer

No book can prevent all dog bites to children. This book is designed to provide information that will help parents do a better job of supervising and managing the interactions between their children and their family dog.

It is sold with the understanding that the publisher and author are not engaged in rendering specific advice and that readers will need to use their judgment or employ the services of a competent dog trainer for additional assistance.

It is not the purpose of this manual to reprint all the information that is otherwise available regarding dog training and parenting, but instead to complement, amplify, and supplement other texts. You are urged to read all the available material, learn as much as possible about canine and human behavior, and tailor the information to your individual needs. For more information, see the many resources in appendix B.

Every effort has been made to make this manual as complete and as accurate as possible. However, there may be mistakes, both typographical and in content. Therefore this text should be used only as a general guide and not as the ultimate source of information for parents with regard to their children and their dog's interaction.

The purpose of this manual is to educate and entertain. The author and Dream Dog Productions, LLC, shall have neither liability nor responsibility to any person or entity with respect to any loss or damage caused, or alleged to have been caused, directly or indirectly, by the information contained in this book.

If you do not wish to be bound by the above, you may return this book to the publisher for a full refund.

Table of Contents

Babies and Toddlers: Coping with Cribs and Kibble   73

Preschoolers: Someone's Always Underfoot   89

Elementary Schoolers: Whose Turn Is It to Feed Edzo?   103

Teens: As If Hormones Weren't Enough   127

Kids & Dogs:
You Can Conquer the Chaos

Kids and dogs. They go together like apple pie and vanilla ice cream or cookies and milk. We expect kids and dogs to get along great and be best buddies. So we might wonder why anyone would need a book about living with kids and dogs.

Once you try having both under the same roof, you know the truth: living with kids and dogs in the same household is not always easy. And most books aren't much help. Parenting books say "control your dog." Dog-training books say "control your kid." The reality is far more complex and goes way beyond placing blame on either children or dogs for being who they are.

 Every year, nearly 2.8 million children are bitten by a dog. Boys are bitten nearly twice as often as girls, and children between 5 and 9 years old are the most at risk. Most of these bites come from a dog that belongs to the family or a friend.

Parents can do a lot to foster a strong, loving relationship between their children and their dog. It's simply a matter of education. We do the best we can with what we know. When we know more, we do better. Let's do better!

What Makes This Book Important

Plenty of books discuss how to prepare your dog for the arrival of a new baby, but why would someone need a book about preparing a dog for living with an older child, or vice versa?

Let's think for a minute about some statistics. According to the Centers for Disease Control, approximately half of all kids under 14 have been bitten by a dog. Kids between 5 and 9 are at the highest risk for a dog bite. Most dogs who bite are between 2 and 4 years old. Do the math. By writing books that only address introducing your adult dog to an infant, we focus on the least potentially dangerous child/dog relationship.

Of course, we need to do everything we can to keep infants safe around dogs. But we also need to recognize that there are safety issues at every age and stage

Stories of dogs running loose and biting children capture the media's attention. Consequently, most people believe that loose dogs pose the greatest risk and that dog bites are unpredictable, freak accidents. Unfortunately such beliefs aren't true. Approximately 61 percent of dog bites to children come from a dog that belongs to the child's family or to a friend.

So, we need to focus inward and look at what we can do in our homes to improve the relationship between our kids and our dogs—information that's missing in both parenting books and dog-training books. Few books in either genre do more than mention casually that parents need to supervise. Parents are trying to supervise. Of course they are! But they don't have all the information they need to do the job right, and that's why this book is important.

It's Not As Easy as It Looks

While dogs may be "man's best friend," the two species differ profoundly from each other. Dogs consider some human behavior to be rude, and humans view some dog behavior as equally unacceptable. Learning more about these differences, especially about normal dog behavior, can help parents to supervise better and to avoid mishaps.

Good kids and good dogs can get into trouble because of miscommunication. Let's say your kids and a few friends are playing tag in the back yard, and you let your border collie, Streak, out to join the game. She'll start rounding those kids up, possibly even by nipping at their ankles. Is she being aggressive? No, she's simply doing what she was bred to do: round up a flock of sheep and bring them to one place. But just as you and the kids don't understand what Streak is doing, the dog doesn't realize what's going on either. She may be alarmed that the "sheep"—in other words, your kids—are screaming and running off in random directions. She needs to understand that this behavior is common—and normal—in children.

GOOD INTENTIONS, POOR RESULTS

The photos below are a great example of miscommunication. To begin, most dogs do not enjoy being petted on the top of the head, and yet people nearly always pet dogs this way. It's better to reach beneath a dog's chin.

This puppy is signalling his discomfort in the only way he knows how—through body language. In the first photo, the puppy is only mildly uncomfortable. His mouth is closed and he's leaning away, but he still has one of his forepaws curled beneath his body.

As the person comes closer, the puppy's discomfort increases. With his mouth still closed, he crouches down to avoid the touch and moves his paw out from beneath his body. In addition, you can see a small cresent of white at the corner of his eyes, which indicates stress.

By the third photo, he's had enough and nips at the person's hand. This kind of bite is often considered unprovoked—after all, the person was bitten for trying to be friendly—but from a dog's point of view, he tried repeatedly to politely say no and the person just kept coming.

Learning to interpret basic body language (both human and canine) is a beneficial skill for every parent.

You will encounter these kinds of miscommunication every day. A dog considers jumping up part of a normal, friendly greeting, but such a greeting can frighten or even injure a child. Similarly, hugging is a sign of human affection, but it makes a dog feel trapped and anxious.

So, who is going to wade into the middle and sort things out? You are! It doesn't have to be an "us versus them" mentality. You can teach your kids how to relate to dogs, and you can gently, without force or fury, teach your dog to understand children.

Dog Training is a Lot Like Parenting

In orientation sessions for my group dog-training classes, I discuss the techniques the families will be using to develop strong relationships with their dogs and to promote good behavior. Invariably, someone will ask, "Does this work for kids too?"

> ### GO WITH YOUR GUT
>
> Sometimes parents tell me that something doesn't feel right. They can't identify a specific problem, just that they are uncomfortable with how their dog interacts with their children.
>
> In almost all of those instances, the parents are right. They see a problem with their dog that goes beyond normal canine exuberance or lack of training.
>
> Trust your instincts. If you are worried, talk to a trainer.

The answer is, "Yes!" The training methods set dogs up for success, reward them for good behavior, and promote two-way communication—just like we do as parents. We use management techniques to keep our children out of mischief and away from danger. We develop relationships in which our children respect us and follow directions (most of the time!), but do not fear us.

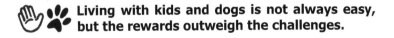 **Living with kids and dogs is not always easy, but the rewards outweigh the challenges.**

Kids and dogs are egocentric. They do what works for them. That's fine. By making things fun, we can teach them both what they need to know. Clear expectations and consistent rules work better in the long run.

Safety Concerns

Many parents tell me, "If my dog ever bites my child, he's out of here!" That's too late! There are lots of early-warning signs that you must be able to identify to prevent dog bites from occurring.

Almost every episode of the television show "America's Funniest Home Videos" features clips that terrify me. Parents happily film incidents in which dogs are growling at children, dragging them by their clothing, or standing frozen and stiff while tolerating something the children are doing. Yikes! With a little more provocation, these dogs could easily bite. But with a little more information, these parents would know that, instead of filming such scenes, they should be stopping them.

It is vital to advocate on behalf of your child and your dog. If you allow troubling behavior to continue, the relationship between your child and dogs (all dogs) will be harmed. Your child may even develop a life-long fear of dogs. I often conduct bite-prevention workshops in preschools and elementary schools where I meet many children who are afraid to approach my dog. That's really sad.

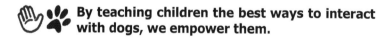 **By teaching children the best ways to interact with dogs, we empower them.**

You can give your children the skills they need to be safe, kind friends to animals. In turn, they will receive all the love and affection that dogs can provide.

The Three Keys to Success

The three most important things you can focus on are relationship, management, and training.

Relationship

Relationship is the reason we acquire dogs in the first place. We want them to be loving members of our families. We want to enjoy spending time with them and sharing our lives with them, and we want them to feel the same way about us. To have a good relationship with anyone, we must be able to communicate with them and they must be able to communicate with us.

Many people mistakenly believe that the communication between a family and their dog is one way: telling the dog what to do. That's only half the equation. For balance, the dog must be able to respond and "talk" to us. When Streak is truly a member of your family, each person will have a unique and special relationship with her, and she with them. Take time to listen to your dog. She really has a lot to say, if you give her the chance.

Management

Parents use management all the time to prevent problems from cropping up. We can't always see them coming, but afterward we can usually see what went wrong. One of the most useful things a parent can do is to analyze problems and create a game plan to avoid recurrences.

- Why did Shawn become whiny at 5:15 p.m.? He was probably hungry. Tomorrow try giving him a small snack at 4:00 p.m. to tide him over until dinner.

- Why does Streak jump up and take things off the counter? Because there's food within her reach. Try to keep the food put away in upper cabinets.

- Why was Streak trying to avoid Samantha? Because Samantha kept trying to put a ribbon on her tail. Giving Samantha a stuffed dog to play dress-up with may help redirect your daughter's energy.

• Why did Streak run around the house, knock things over, and chew on the kitchen chairs? She needed more exercise. Give her an outlet for all that energy, and she'll be calmer in the house.

Most problems that parents encounter can be resolved through training, but an equal number can be avoided altogether through management. Decide how you want to focus your energy.

TAGGING GOOD BEHAVIOR

To learn quickly, dogs need to know precisely when they do something right. One way to impart that knowledge is tag and reward specific behaviors. This way dogs learn to offer us more of the things we like and less of what we don't.

We use clickers in my group classes. These small, handheld noisemakers create a distinctive sound that owners use when their dogs do something right. Dogs quickly learn that when they hear the click, they have earned a treat.

It's asking a lot, though, to have busy parents carry around a piece of dog-training equipment, even a small one. If that's your situation, what could you do instead?

You could simply praise your dog, but that's much tougher for dogs to figure out. Because praise often involves varied words and tones, your message may be unclear to your dog. Here's my compromise: Click with your tongue. This click is always available and won't be laden down like your hands. And it's a distinct sound, instead of a word, which makes the signal clear for your dog. I use the tongue click frequently when I don't have a clicker ready and I want to tell a dog she's made a good choice.

Throughout the book, I will say "click and give the dog a treat." Always make your designated noise first, then follow it with a treat. The click is the equivalent of flashing lights and ringing bells on a game show. "Congratulations! You have just won a fabulous prize! Let's see what it is. Oh, look! It's a piece of cheddar cheese! Oh, you lucky dog!"

The chapters that follow offer many specific suggestions for managing situations to prevent problems. Chapter 5 discusses equipment—such as baby gates and walking harnesses—that can help in your day-to-day life.

Training

I am a dog trainer, so I absolutely recognize the power and benefit of training. But I also believe that training belongs third among the three keys to success.

Parents are busy, and dogs can be a lot of work. By focusing first on developing a strong relationship and then looking at ways to prevent problems, having a dog will be more enjoy-

---

FINDING A GOOD TRAINER

The best dog trainers are as good with people as they are with dogs. (A few trainers forget the human side of the equation.)

The Association of Pet Dog Trainers (APDT) maintains a database that you can search to find a trainer in your area: www.apdt.com. APDT promotes dog-friendly training methods and continuing education, but not all members are equally dog friendly. Be sure to interview a trainer before hiring.

Certified Pet Dog Trainers (CPDTs) have over 300 hours of training experience and have passed a nationally administered exam. The exam's five content areas include learning theory, instruction skills, husbandry, ethology, and equipment. You can find a trainer with a CPDT title at the Certification Council for Professional Dog Trainers website: www.ccpdt.com. CPDTs are required to earn continuing education credits to maintain their certification.

The International Association of Animal Behavior Consultants is a professional association for the field of animal behavior consulting and facilitates research, theory development, and education. To find a certified or associate member, go to www.iaabc.org.

Talk to the trainer about his or her training techniques. If the trainer offers group classes, ask if you can come observe a lesson to see if the teaching style is a good fit for your family. Make certain that the trainer understands that you want your dog to be a full member of a family that includes children.

able. This is critically important. If the parents don't enjoy having Streak around, if she becomes "more trouble than she's worth," a whole new set of problems arise.

 Once you have a strong relationship and good management skills, dog training becomes fun, not another burden on your "to do" list.

Look for a trainer who offers fun classes and welcomes family participation. It's important that the whole family learn how to interact with Streak, not just you. For this reason, you should avoid training that relies on confrontation or the use of force. While you may be able to physically manipulate or socially intimidate your dog into behaving, your child cannot and should not.

Modern training methods—properly applied—work well for everyone. These methods rely on rewarding the dog for doing the right thing and redirecting or ignoring the dog when he does the wrong thing. These methods enable Streak to listen to and respond to cues given by both you and your children. However, because kids are inconsistent and still learning, you should not hold Streak to the same standard of obedience with your kids as you do with your-self.

About the Book

As you can see, this book doesn't concentrate exclusively on dog training. Many excellent dog-training books are available, but none of them provide the information that a parent needs to promote loving relationships between their children and their dog.

This book does much more than simply tell parents to supervise their children around dogs and vice versa. The book provides easy-to-implement advice and clear descriptions of normal child and canine behavior. I've organized the book to cover the spectrum of what you will encounter in your children's lives:

- Chapter 2 tells you what to look for in a good family dog.
- Chapter 3 covers bite prevention and canine body language in detail.
- Chapter 4 discusses some behavior issues that can be hard to deal with in a household that includes children.
- Chapter 5 lists some equipment that you may find useful as well as some things you may want to avoid.
- Chapters 6 through 9 cover specific age ranges of children: infants and toddlers, preschoolers, elementary schoolers, and teens.
- Chapter 10 is the sad stuff—helping your child deal with life without your dog.

Each chapter names a child and a dog. Because children and dogs can be either male or female, I alternated genders by chapter. For simplicity's sake and ease of reading, in most cases, I assigned the child one gender and the dog the other.

Words for the Weary

Too tired to read the whole chapter? Hit the highlights! Each chapter ends with a condensed version of the most important points. Here are the themes you should carry away from this chapter.

- Living with kids and dogs is not always easy, but the rewards can be great.
- There are many parallels between parenting and raising a dog.
- Relationship, management, and training are the keys to success in helping children and dogs live together.
- You must act as an advocate for both your child and your dog to ensure all interactions are safe, kind, and fun.
- We empower our children and keep them safer by teaching them the best ways to interact with dogs.

Best Friend or Bad Choice: The Right Dog for Your Family

Should We Get a Dog?

Nearly every parent has to answer that question sooner or later. Coming up with the answer involves a very big decision that shouldn't be made lightly.

Getting a dog is a long-term commitment to having another living, breathing, eating, mess-making member of the family. Just as no two people are alike, no two dogs are alike either. You must consider which characteristics you can live with in a dog and which ones you cannot.

The first and most important question to answer is, why would we want to add a dog to our family? There is no perfect answer to this question. The best answers have to do with enjoying spending time with dogs and loving the companionship they provide.

Do you want a dog? Answer honestly. There's a big difference between wanting a dog and wanting to get a dog for your kids. Parents must take the ultimate responsibility for any pet, and a dog is a lot more work than a gerbil.

Be sure that you are willing to commit the time, money, and energy to having a dog so that you don't wind up feeling like a martyr when dog care duties inevitably fall to you. Don't fall for your kids' earnest faces and pleading promises to care for the dog. Make no mistake—regardless of what they say now—you will be the one who makes sure Shadow's needs are met.

Dogs are a lot of work and can cost a lot of money. Current studies indicate that dog ownership costs between $500 to $1,000 per year. You'll need to consider all the tasks and costs associated with a dog, such as food, walking, cleanup, grooming, veterinary care, beds, toys, and possible damage from chewing or housetraining accidents, etc.

Kids have no idea what responsible dog ownership requires. By all means, assign them responsibilities for caring for the dog, but know that you'll need to follow behind to ensure all the tasks are done—just like you did for all the other skills they needed to master. And don't tell the kids that if they don't take care of the dog, you'll get rid of him. Such threats place an unfair burden on your children. Think of all the years they'll spend telling their psychotherapist about how their parents gave Shadow away because they kept forgetting to fill his water bowl!

Does your family have any special circumstances that should be taken into account? If you have your hands full caring for three kids under the age of 6, are you ready to take on more work? Do any of your kids have special needs that might make

PERHAPS A CAT?

Social cats can make wonderful family pets—and they are easier to care for than dogs. Cats can also be trained using the same positive-reinforcement techniques that we use for dogs.

Ask to meet some friendly cats at your local shelter. Some of them are true extroverts and would love to join your family.

having a dog more challenging? Do you have an active schedule that keeps you away from the house for many hours each day? Carefully analyze how your life will be affected by adding a dog to your family.

If you don't already have a dog, it might be best to wait until your youngest child is at least 5 years old. Children younger than 5 don't really understand how to be fair and kind to dogs; it's up to their parents to model appropriate behavior and to closely supervise all of their interactions with the family pets.

You can't live without a dog? Me neither. But in that case, understand that you are choosing a dog for your own reasons, not for the kids. It needs to be a safe dog for your kids, of course, but you are choosing to have a dog because you want a dog. I've often told people that I know life could be easier without a dog, but, for me, it could never be better without one.

What Breed of Dog Should We Get?

When asked what breed of dog I recommend for families with young kids, I've been known to answer, "Whatever Mom wants." That's sexist—I know, I know! But the question is a lot tougher than it sounds. Many moms wind up shouldering most of the dog duties (and scooping most of the dog doody too). If she wants "little, white, and fluffy" and the kids want "large and boisterous," a realistic look at the situation is called for.

I've known some wonderful moms who came regularly to training with the dogs their children chose. One particularly memorable family included a pit bull named Lester. Lester was a lovable lug, but he was strong and goofy. One of Tammy's teenage sons had brought him home and asked to keep him. Tammy was very

SHOULD WE GET A DOG?
ONE TIME WHEN THE ANSWER SHOULD BE "NO"

If your child is afraid of dogs, work on that fear first, before adding a dog to your household.

Parents are often told that getting a puppy and raising it with the child will help the child get over her fear of dogs. That's not always true. Puppies are boisterous and nippy. If your child is already worried about dogs, she really won't like having 22 pounds of fluff launch itself at her.

IMPORTANT

Start by introducing older, calm dogs to your child. Respect her fear and work at her own pace. Talk with her about the dogs you see. Learn about dog body language so that you can interpret for her what the dogs are communicating. You may want to start with books or videos first. Then have her watch (from a spot where she feels safe) as you and/or other kids interact with a dog.

Most children will reach out and touch a calm dog's haunches if the owner turns the dog's head away from the child. That's an excellent first step. Talk with your child about how the dog's fur feels. Ask her if she thinks other dogs' fur would be softer or rougher. Get her thinking about that one dog as an individual.

Work toward having her give the dog cues (with dog's owner ensuring that the dog complies). Seeing a dog respond correctly to what she asks will help her feel safer.

It's best for her to work steadily with one dog until she feels very comfortable before adding another. Once she has met and likes three calm, adult dogs, begin thinking about introducing her to a puppy.

Let her start out at a distance, simply observing the puppy's behavior. Talk with her about the ways in which the puppy is similar to and different from the adult dogs she's met. When she is ready, let her approach the puppy. Be sure that adults are there to prevent the puppy from jumping on her; that would set your progress back considerably. Give her treats that she can toss away from herself for the puppy to eat.

If she's ready, teach her how to lure the puppy into a sit. First, show her how holding a treat in your hand and moving it just barely higher than the puppy's nose in the direction of his tail will cause the puppy to lift his head up and put his haunches down. Do it a few times so she can watch you. Then have her put a treat in her fist and wrap your hand around hers and lure the puppy into a sit. (Still have an adult there to prevent jumping.)

IMPORTANT Take it slow. It's much better to teach your child to be a skilled observer of animal behavior than it is for her to be thrown into situations that frighten her.

diligent about coming to class; we saw her every week as she learned how to handle this bouncy dog who had very little self-control. But I never met any of her four teens, not even the 18-year-old son who was officially Lester's owner.

Another mom comes to class with her two young sons and the family's Labrador retriever mix, Nelly. At home, Nelly is gentle, calm, and kind. In the presence of other dogs, such as at the vet's office and on walks, she is revved up, barky, and prone to lunging at any other dog she encounters. Cathy's well-mannered kids wait in the office during class because it really isn't safe for them to be standing close to their mom as she learns to help Nelly deal with her dog-to-dog aggression issues. Cathy has told me that she's considered giving Nelly up, but she knows it would make her sons sad. She's right, but that certainly puts her in a bad position.

When choosing a dog for your family, breed is not necessarily the best factor to rely on. Mixed-breed dogs are often both physically and emotionally healthier than many pure-bred dogs. Think about your "perfect dog." What does he act like? Does this image match the "perfect dogs" chosen by the rest of your family? Have everyone in your family write down the three characteristics that are most important to them (e.g., friendly, energetic, big, small, jogging partner, fluffy, cuddly, short hair). Then compare and narrow down your list to identify the three or four most important characteristics for your family.

Look for a dog that meets many of the criteria on your be-havior wish list. Be prepared to compromise on breed and physical characteristics. The perfect dog for you may come in a much different "package" than you were initially expect-ing. It's not a beauty contest—it's a personality contest. You want Miss Congeniality, not Miss Best in Show! In the end, you will love a dog that fits well into your family, not the dog that looks the way you think he should.

 You are far better off looking for specific behavior traits than choosing a dog based on the reputation of its breed(s).

When talking with families about choosing a dog, I often draw a parallel to my family. I have three sons. These boys have the same parents, same household, same rules, same food, same environment, same, same, same. Therefore, I should have three boys who are very similar, right? Not even close. My guys span the gamut from extroverted to a little shy to quite introverted. How could this be?

The answer is temperament. Genes play a big role in de-termining what a dog's temperament is, and the many ways that genes can combine ensures that every litter of puppies will span the same behavioral spectrum that my sons do. So, the fact that a breed has the reputation of being good with kids doesn't guarantee that all puppies in that breed will be equally child friendly. In other words, you can't choose just any puppy from the litter and assume that he'll fit into your family well. You need to assess each individual puppy to determine which pup's temperament is best for your fam-ily.

SO YOU WANT A SMART DOG . . .

People often choose a dog breed because they've seen it on a list of smartest breeds. But high intelligence may not be the smartest criteria to use if you're choosing a family dog. The up side of these breeds is that they are packed with personality, excited about learning, and show a zest for life.

The down side is that they must have a job to do. Don't have a flock of sheep? Then you may not want a border collie, who probably will substitute your children for woolies to herd. In other words, if you don't find ways for these dogs to channel their boundless physical and mental energy, they'll come up with something on their own.

These are the kinds of dogs who learn to empty your garbage can whenever you answer your phone. They are always alert for opportunities—to take a sandwich off the counter, to bolt out an open door, to open packages left within their reach. Their intelligence and problem-solving ability is exactly what makes them challenging pets.

Don't get me wrong! These are not bad dogs; they are smart dogs! So decide for yourself whether you are mentally agile enough to keep up with this kind of dog and whether you are excited about doing the training you'll need to keep these dogs too busy to find their own fun.

Sad to say, I am not smarter than a Jack Russell Terrier. I love them in class, but they're not the right dog for my home.

Here's my nonscientific top 10 list of commonly seen, busy, bright breeds, listed alphabetically. Think long and hard before choosing one of these dogs for your family.

- Australian Cattle Dog
- Australian Shepherd
- Belgians: Malinois, Tervuren, and Sheepdog
- Border Collie
- Cairn Terrier
- Dalmatian
- Jack Russell Terrier
- Pit Bull Terrier/American Staffordshire Terrier
- Siberian Husky
- Weimaraner

What to Look for in a Good Family Dog

Long ago I attended a dog-training conference at which the speaker said, "There's no such thing as the perfect dog." This started a bit of mumbling in the audience, which she interrupted by saying, "Oh, I know some of you think you have the perfect dog, but I guarantee you . . . that dog is over 5 and you have learned to compromise!" So true.

Choosing a family dog is a lot like choosing a new house. You may like the kitchen in one house, the yard of another, and the location of a third, but you are unable to assemble the bits and pieces into your dream home. You need to make some compromises.

Here's a list of "must have" characteristics for your dog:

• Friendly and social

• Will not guard food, toys, or other objects

• Energy level compatible with your family's and with the amount of time your family has to spend with the dog

You can compromise on some other aspects. The perfect dog for you may not be at all what you initially imagined.

Extroverts Only

A good family dog loves people, especially kids. That cannot be overstated. It's the most important trait to look for. If Shadow loves people, then he'll assume that someone stepping on his tail did so accidentally, not to attack him. Kids in particular really need this canine benefit of the doubt. (Occasionally children will deliberately do something unkind to Shadow. In these cases, refer to the age-appropriate chapter for advice on how to handle the situation.)

 A good family dog loves people, especially kids.

Accidents happen all the time. My kids have dropped things on my dog, fallen over him, stepped on his toes and tail, thrown toys that have hit him (but were not thrown at him), driven radio-controlled cars into him, and jumped over him when racing through the house. Not one of those things was an intentional assault on the dog, but they happened. And they happened in a household where the mom was actively supervising and emphasizing fairness to the dog.

Does that list sound extreme? Probably not if you are the parent of a child 5 or older. Reality is chaotic, messy, and loud. You'll want a dog who can handle it with aplomb.

Good kids and good dogs will still have misunderstandings—every day.

No Resource Guarding

Many dogs covet items they value such as food, toys, or chewies. They'll hover over them, freeze, stare, growl, snap, or even bite if you try to take such items from them. To a certain extent, this can be considered normal behavior—animals need to protect their food sources in order to survive—but there are wide ranges in dogs' reactions. The best family dogs will easily surrender anything in their possession.

Family life is full of unexpected occurrences. Once my son Brandon put Gordo's dish by the glass-fronted storm door not far from where I was working on the computer. Gordo was happily eating in full view of the neighborhood children when suddenly Brandon decided to open the door to let a new 5-year-old neighbor pet Gordo.

A Closer Look Reveals...

This dog is guarding her toy by hovering over it with stiff body language. She is also showing half-moon eyes.

"Brandon, don't let someone pet Gordo while he's eating," I called, and so Brandon let go of the storm door, grabbed the food bowl, and moved it closer to my desk. Gordo merely followed behind, happy to be fed wherever food appeared and regardless of who might be touching him at the time.

THICK OR THIN?

Have you ever thought about the difference between an Arabian horse and a Clydesdale? How about the difference between a sheltie and a bulldog? A giraffe versus an elephant?

Recent research indicates that body type may have an effect on behavior. Animals with thinner bone structure tend to be more skittish and active. Animals with sturdy, stocky builds are likely to be more placid.

While certain breeds of dogs are known for thick or thin bone structures, this seems to hold true within the breed as well. Beagles, for example, can range from very fine boned to quite solid.

Choose your dog based on the behavioral traits you most desire. Looking at body type may help you narrow your search, but should not be the deciding factor.

That could have been a situation in which two young boys were bitten. It was a management failure on my part; I simply hadn't anticipated that Brandon would open the door, and he knows not to move the bowl while Gordo is eating, but in this instance he forgot. Lots of things happen that you just don't anticipate. It had never happened before, so we'd never discussed it. But nothing bad happened because Gordo doesn't growl or bite over food. How fortunate for all of us.

That's why you want a dog with good social skills and no resource-guarding issues. Chapter 4 discusses resource guarding in more detail.

Energy Level

Some dogs are couch potatoes, while others seem to operate only in high gear. What is your family's activity level? Are you in perpetual motion or more fond of board games around the coffee table? Be sure to look for a dog whose energy level matches yours.

All dog breeds were created to fill specific needs: tending livestock, guarding property, scenting prey, retrieving fowl, and killing rodents to name a few. Many of these dogs live to work and need a challenge. Ask whether the dog comes from "field lines" or "show lines." Dogs with field backgrounds are usually significantly more active than their show brethren. Within a breed, there can be large differences.

I know three Labradors—Sabre, Denver, and Gordo—who run a gamut of activity levels. Sabre gets about 6 miles of walking per day and she will retrieve a ball for hours on end. Denver enjoys about an hour of walking, swimming, or jogging each day, and he'll retrieve a ball for more than an hour. Gordo is fond of napping and will occasionally run behind other dogs in the general direction of the ball. Which dog would be best in your house? Talk to the breeder, shelter personnel, or rescue volunteer about the energy level of the dog you are considering.

TIME TO CALL IN THE PROS?

If all else fails, you may want to consider sending your dog to a good doggie daycare once or twice a week, setting up play dates with neighbors' dogs, or hiring a dog walker. By getting worn out elsewhere, he may learn the joy of snoozing at home. See appendix B for more information about how to find a good daycare.

Even if you do get a dog who seems "hyper," there are things you can do. It's common for people to say that their dog has Attention Deficit/Hyperactivity Disorder (ADHD), and I believe them. But in many of those cases, the problem can be resolved by feeding the dog a high-quality food that does not include any corn, providing adequate exercise, and rewarding the dog for calm behavior.

I sometimes jokingly say that I would like to play a mix-and-match game with some of the dogs and families that come to my classes. I see lots of low-key dogs in go-go-go homes and far too many live-wire dogs who live with couch potatoes. It's my silly fantasy to rearrange some of these matches. In many cases, I believe both the families and the dogs would be happier with the better-fitting partner.

PET STORES AND INTERNET PUPPIES

Please don't buy a dog from a pet store or from a breeder over the Internet. Most of these dogs have not had the best start in life. Many are excessively shy, which is never a good trait for a dog that lives with kids. Housetraining issues are common because the pups and their mother were not able to stay clean, so they don't learn not to soil their living spaces. It is quite common for these puppies to have respiratory infections or other illnesses.

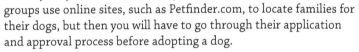

The best breeders, shelters, and rescue groups would not consider sending a dog to a family they have not met. Many of these groups use online sites, such as Petfinder.com, to locate families for their dogs, but then you will have to go through their application and approval process before adopting a dog.

There are lots of wonderful dogs in your area that need homes. Ask someone qualified in behavior assessment to help you choose the right dog for your family (see appendix B). Don't risk it on the luck of the draw.

Little Dogs, Big Concerns

Avoid getting a very small dog for a family with children. Dogs less than 20 pounds are fragile and too easy for kids to pick up. Children are tempted to carry these dogs around like toys. Do not allow your children to pick up or carry any dog. Instead, have them sit on the floor and encourage the dog to come onto their lap.

When dogs are carried, they often feel unsteady and insecure, so they may wiggle and try to get away. If your child puts Shadow down each time he squirms, the dog is learning that being held feels unsafe and that active resistance is the best defense. Over time, this could result in Shadow becoming snappish whenever he is picked up.

Don't let this behavior pattern start. Create a family rule that only adults can pick up the dog, regardless of the dog's size.

TEMPERAMENT TESTING

Many shelters and rescue groups now perform temperament tests on their dogs to help find the best families for them.

The two most important components of a temperament test for a family dog are checking for a strong social drive and a lack of resource guarding. Ask questions about how each dog performed.

If your shelter or rescue group does not test for these traits, ask if you can bring a trainer in to assess the dog. Peace of mind is worth the price.

Adult or Puppy?

Most people plan to get a puppy, but there are lots of good reasons to consider an older dog. You'll need to decide what is right for your family.

Puppies are cute, fun—and so much work! There's housetraining, bite inhibition, puppy-proofing and socialization, for starters.

Socialization—the process of helping your puppy become comfortable with the sights, sounds, and other experiences of life with human beings—is your most important job.

Try to give your puppy as many new positive experiences as possible so that he'll be comfortable in any setting as he ages. Use lots of treats to keep your puppy happy and

IS SANTA SCARY?

When asked to sit on Santa's lap, many children are afraid—and understandably so.

Socialization, that same process that helps puppies learn about the world, applies to people too. Very few children encounter men who look, dress, and act like Santa on a regular basis. The unknown is scary!

When evaluating kid-and-dog interactions, I often caution parents to be sure to look at both sides of the equation. Good intentions don't count for much when the recipient is uncomfortable.

I'm sure Santa's not trying to frighten these children, but clearly this a moment when a caring parent should step in and end the interaction rather than trying to force things along.

Similarly, when your child or your dog shows discomfort, first solve the stress. Later you can step back and make a plan to ensure that the next encounter is fun for everyone.

secure, and be careful not to overwhelm your pup with too much, too soon. Be sure that he meets at least 100 people by the time he's 16 weeks old, from babies to senior citizens. This will help him to be friendly and social throughout his life.

With a puppy, you will also need to teach bite inhibition and housetraining. These topics are covered in chapters 3 and 4. (See chapter 5 for information about puppy-proofing.)

With older dogs, for the most part, what you see is what you get. You can see how they react to children, other dogs, cats, unusual noises, etc. Many adult dogs are already housetrained.

People often worry that older dogs are somehow "damaged goods." That is simply not true for many of the dogs in shelters and rescue groups. Dogs are sometimes given up for reasons unrelated to their behavior, such as divorce, moving, increased work schedules, and allergies. There are countless wonderful dogs in need of good homes. Take your time finding just the right dog for your family; this is a long-term decision.

Ask your friends and neighbors where they got their dog, who their vet is, and which trainer they use—and then ask how happy they are with the services of each. Shelter workers, breeders, veterinarians, and trainers can help you decide what behavioral traits best suit your family's needs. (Vets and trainers may be the best sources of objective advice. Because they are the least likely to have their own reasons for encouraging adoption of any specific dog, they are apt to help you select a dog based specifically on criteria that are in your family's best interest.) Give the experts a chance to help you before you get a dog, so that you'll never wish you could play my mix-and-match game.

Spaying and Neutering Your Pet

It's always a good idea to spay or neuter your dog. There are many health and behavioral benefits to each procedure including a decrease in aggression, roaming, and marking (i.e., urinating on every vertical surface), and prevention of cancer in the reproductive organs.

For male dogs, neutering greatly reduces the incidence of marking, roaming, and mounting (pre-mating displays). Also keep in mind that intact male dogs have the highest number of bites toward children. It's just not worth the risk.

You already have a busy life. Do you really want to add the complications of caring for your dog through pregnancy and 8 weeks of puppyhood? The miracle of birth is all well and good, but most kids' reaction is, "Oh, gross." Then, 8 weeks later, they are so bonded to the puppies that they can hardly bear to see them go.

 Good family dogs are worth their weight in gold.

Evaluating the Dog You Already Have

Most of the families I see already have a dog. Many couples adopt a dog a few years before they plan to have children. These dogs need help adjusting to the big changes that children bring.

Another common scenario is for families to get a dog when their youngest child enters preschool or kindergarten. The parents want their kids to grow up with a dog and now have enough energy to consider adding one to the family.

These are two very different scenarios; I lived them both. When my first child was born, we had a 2-year-old golden retriever. Midas was a happy-go-lucky, social, easily excited dog. (She also ate poor-quality food, but I didn't know any better then.) While she adored my son (and the two that followed), she was well aware that life had changed—not necessarily for the better at times.

She was in the midst of everything, snuffling up cracker crumbs from the baseboards, nosing her way into diaper

 pails (more on that in chapter 5), and gently evading children crawling toward her as fast as they could. When all of the children would be in bed, she would usually come over to me, lay her head on my knee, and let out a contented sigh before curling up on the floor at my feet.

GARBAGE IN, GARBAGE OUT?

I am a believer in the benefits of a high-quality diet for dogs. While I am by no means an expert on the subject, I have seen countless dogs' behavior and health improve when they are switched to foods that do not have dyes, artificial preservatives, or ground yellow corn.

There is no one dog food that is perfect for all dogs. Each dog, just like each person, has unique physical needs. Think about it—if you and I ate the same food every day, would we be equally healthy? Of course not. One of us would do a bit better than the other.

Consequently, I believe in changing dog foods each year. I always choose one of the foods recommended by Whole Dog  Journal (my favorite dog magazine, it's like Consumer Reports for dog lovers). Each year in September, when the kids get a new teacher, I begin the transition to a new dog food. (Some people switch quarterly, but that's too much hassle for me.) This way, over the course of the dog's life, I hope to have met all of his nutritional needs, providing neither an excess nor deficiency of any nutrients.

Gordo stepped right into a chaotic household. When he arrived, the boys were 2, 4, and 7. He has no idea that some houses don't have remote-control cars racing down the hallways, toys strewn everywhere, or children who run in and out all day long. This is his reality; it's all he's ever known.

You might think that Gordo would be the dog who'd seek me out during the quiet times, but he is so used to sharing my attention that he doesn't really act any different whether the kids are there or not. Midas went from being the dog who went everywhere with me to being left home when I couldn't juggle more than an infant car seat, a diaper bag, and a wayward toddler.

Questions to Consider About Your Dog

Take a good look at Shadow. To help manage all the interactions between your kids and your dog, it's important that you look at your dog objectively, which is easier said than done.

How social is Shadow? Does he seek out human interaction or just tolerate it when it's forced upon him? Does he have any sensitive spots on his body? Any place he doesn't want you to touch? Does he have any medical concerns that might cause him discomfort?

Has Shadow been around kids for large blocks of time? Strangers meeting him at the pet store don't count. How about nieces and nephews who come over and stay for hours or even days? Is he tired by the end? Does he look for a way to get away or show stress signals such as lip-licking, yawning, or turning away? (Always, always provide your dog a place where he can go to be alone and recharge.) Is he more interested in the adults than the kids? Great family dogs don't just tolerate kids, they love them.

How good is his obedience? Does Shadow usually come when you call him? Can you get him to stop barking when you ask?

Most important, have you ever (not just in connection with kids) seen any of the warning signs that dogs give when they are very uncomfortable: frozen posture, hard stare, curled lip, or growling?

Answering these questions will give you a fairly objective assessment of Shadow's behavior and will help you a lot as you supervise your kids with him. If you know that he is uncomfortable when he can't easily walk away, you'll make sure that the living room is not so strewn with baby equipment that his options become limited. If you know that Shadow loves playing with kids for about 30 minutes and then needs a break, you'll learn to keep an eye on the clock—and his behavior—and will call him away for a rest period after about 20 minutes. Always leave him wanting more.

Take your dog to a group training class. Behavior deteriorates under stress; this will give you a good indication of how well your dog will listen when . . . the baby arrives, your mother-in-law visits, or you throw a Scooby Doo party for seven 5-year-olds. Training Shadow in a distracting environment, as provided by a good group class, will teach you the tools you need to gain and maintain control over your dog when the unexpected occurs. And all parents know to expect the unexpected.

How a Trainer Can Help

A good trainer can help in many ways. If you do not have a dog already, I strongly recommend you talk to a trainer before choosing. The trainer will be able to help you figure out what behavior traits are best for your family and can point you toward the best shelters, rescue groups, and breeders in the area.

If your dog doesn't quite match your wish list of traits, a trainer can also help you balance your wishes with the reality of the dog, or suggest ways to use all three keys to success: relationship, management, and training.

Words for the Weary

Too tired to read the whole chapter? Hit the highlights!

• Only get a dog if you want one. After all, you will wind up with most of the responsibility.

• Don't get a dog if your child is afraid of dogs.

• You are far better off looking for specific behavior traits than choosing a dog based on the reputation of its breed(s).

- The best family dogs are social and outgoing, and they do not show signs of resource guarding.
- Very small dogs are often too fragile for homes with children.
- Puppies are a lot of work. Don't rule out adult dogs.
- Looking at your dog objectively (using the questions in this chapter) will help you to supervise better and to know when you must intervene.

Preventing Dog Bites: Every Parent's Concern

Each year, approximately 2.8 million children are bitten by a dog. Boys receive two-thirds of these bites. Sixty-one percent of these bites occur in a familiar setting—at home or at a friend or relative's home. But most of these bites can be prevented, if the parents focus on relationship, management, and training.

 Learning to recognize when your dog needs assistance is the best way to avoid problems.

Whenever a child visits our home, I actively supervise every interaction between the dog and the kids (mine too). If I can't supervise, I put Gordo in his crate or behind a baby gate, so that he and the kids are separated.

Kids are exciting and exhausting. All parents know that, but we often forget that our dogs see kids that way too. Dogs become accustomed to the antics of "their" kids, but other children can be very hard for them to read.

Dogs communicate almost entirely through body language. Vocalizations are a very small part of their repertoire, and yet that's what most of us imagine when we think of how dogs interact with each other and with us. And we're much the same: we communicate through body language far more than we realize. However, it is important to learn that our body language can affect our dogs in unexpected (to us) ways.

I find a Wizard of Oz analogy helpful when I'm trying to explain to people how human body language affects dogs. Men are like the tin man; they stand up straight and approach directly. They frequent-

---

DOGGONESAFE.COM'S SUPERVISION GUIDELINES

Many parents wonder when a child is old enough to interact with or walk a dog without supervision. Unfortunately there is no "one size fits all" rule. You are going to have to evaluate both your child and your dog to decide when the time is right.

DoggoneSafe.com suggests

- When the child can read the dog's body language
- When the child and dog have a mutually respectful relationship
- When the dog will happily and willingly follow directions from the child
- If the dog has never shown any sign of aggression toward people or other dogs and does not chase cars, cats, or other animals
- When the child knows how to interpret situations and take appropriate action.

Most kids under 12 will not meet these criteria.

---

ly reach right for the dog's face. Many dogs are intimidated by this frontal advance.

Women are like the scarecrow. We soften our body language by crouching down to make ourselves smaller and less intimidating, and we frequently beckon dogs to approach us, rather than move into their space.

Children are the cowardly lion, and they can be the most frightening of all. They reach forward to pet a dog, then jerk their hand back because they're unsure. Over and over. The dog, watching a hand volley back and forth over his head, often interprets this as teasing. "Can you get me? Here I am! Ha, ha, now I'm gone."

None of these behavioral styles causes aggression in dogs, but if a dog is already uncomfortable and you act like the tin man or the cowardly lion, you only heighten that discomfort.

Parents play a huge role in keeping children safe around dogs. We can do better!

The most important thing we as parents can do is learn a little bit about dogs and their body language. Once we understand what a dog is trying to tell us, we'll be much better equipped to help our dogs and kids understand one another. (See "Three Steps for Meeting a Dog" on pages 111-113.)

Dogs are very adept at reading nonverbal messages from both other dogs and their human families. Unfortunately we often misunderstand or simply don't notice what Liffey is trying to tell us. In my dog-training classes, I frequently stop the class to narrate the messages various dogs are sending with their body language.

For example, dogs display certain mannerisms when they are stressed. These behaviors serve two purposes: they are an attempt at self-soothing, akin to thumb sucking, as well as a message to others that the dog would like the situation to defuse.

These are signs that Liffey is uncomfortable. If she is, you will want to remove her from the situation or have the kids back up and give her more space.

The "Good Dogs" Myth

Many people have the mistaken belief that good dogs don't bite. Reality is more complex.

Good parents never lose their cool. Can we all agree on that? Not really. Some-

times we get in over our heads. We've all had stressful days where we reacted badly. Stress causes our behavior to deteriorate. The same is true of our dogs.

A better maxim would be that dogs don't bite

PLEASE DON'T PUNISH GROWLING!

Growling is an early-warning sign. Warnings are good, not bad! Would you like traffic lights to go from green to red without the yellow? Imagine all the accidents that would cause.

That's similar to what may happen if you punish your dog for growling. You'll teach her that you don't like advance notice and that she cannot count on you for assistance. What you'll find is that she really will begin to bite "suddenly, without warning."

without provocation. Even that one is a little sticky because people don't always recognize what the dog was worrying about. It's not uncommon for people to say that Liffey bit "out of the blue" or "suddenly, without warning." Yet upon review of the circumstances, they can usually see what the trigger was. (Ah, the beauty of hindsight.)

This is why parental supervision and knowledge are so important. Parents who recognize what Liffey is saying will know when to intervene. Every parent learns to recognize the signs that their kids are getting too wild. You'll call, "Hey, guys, settle down. Someone's going to get hurt." If they don't settle down, sure enough, 2 minutes later, someone is crying.

The same is true with dogs. You will notice that the intensity level is rising. That is your cue to step in and calm everyone down. Remember, if Liffey gets revved up and wants to grab onto something, she'll use her teeth. This kind of problem is frustrating, predictable, and avoidable. Keeping their games on a lower energy level is the best course of action.

The Behavior Continuum

No one is ridiculously happy all the time, and yet that's how many people think of dogs. This can put an unfair burden on them.

By looking at dog behavior simply as aggressive (bad) or nonaggressive (good), we allow many improper interactions to occur. Instead I encourage people to divide their dog's behavior into three categories like a traffic light:

- **Enjoyment (green light).** Things are going well. Continue supervising, but there is no need to intervene at this moment.

- **Tolerance (yellow light).** Things are a bit tense. See what you can do to improve the situation. You may need to end the interaction.

- **Enough Already (red light).** Intervene immediately. Give the kids and dogs some time apart.

There's a lot we can do to help a tolerant dog enjoy children more, but there's far less wiggle room between Tolerance and Enough Already. Clearly aggression falls into the Enough Already category, but escape and avoidance be-

---

PUPPIES NEED THEIR MOM'S GUIDANCE

Do not adopt a puppy that was separated from her mother and siblings before 8 weeks.

Between 6-1/2 and 8 weeks, a puppy begins learning about bite inhibition by playing—sometimes too roughly—with her littermates. She'll be told that no one wants to play with her when she hurts them.

If a puppy misses out on this critical stage, she may never fully learn to properly inhibit the intensity of her biting. You will continue her instruction at home, but it's best if she gets her initial lessons from members of her own canine family.

COMMONLY OVERLOOKED STRESS SIGNALS

Although people are told to supervise their dog around children and in new situations, it is rare for them to be taught to look for specific body language signs. These six signals all fall in the yellow zone of Tolerance.

Half-Moon Eye. When a dog is calm and relaxed, you don't usually see much white around her eyes. The "half moon" refers to the white arc that is often seen when a dog is stressed and trying to hold it together.

Shaking Off. I compare this to a reset button. The dog is doing shake off, as if she were wet. It often happens just after a stressful interaction. Pay attention. It happens more often than you might expect. Reboot!

Turning Away. This is as a dog's very polite way of saying, "No, thank you." Be sure to give your dog a break when you see her turning away from the kids because if they don't respond to her polite request, she may respond more rudely the next time.

Consider these signals a call to action. When you see your dog showing any of these stress signals, it may be time to step in.

Early intervention is the key to preventing problems. If you don't take action until your dog is showing more overt signals, the relationship between your kids and the dog will be damaged.

Closed Mouth. It's easy to tell which dog is happier in this picture. When dogs are happy and relaxed, their mouths are typically slightly open. During uncomfortable moments, the mouth closes. This is a great signal for kids to look for when asking permission to pet a dog.

Lip Licking. When a dog is anxious, she will often stick out her tongue and lick her lips. It's usually just a fast, little flick. Watch your dog; this is one of the most common signals. I call it the canine equivalent of thumb sucking.

Yawning. This if often mistaken for contentment. The dog is surrounded by children and she lets out a big yawn. Isn't that sweet? Nope, it's a sign that she's in over her head and would appreciate your help.

DON'T TRY THIS AT HOME

Force-based methods for reducing mouthing may teach your dog to fear you and may actually trigger a bite.

Some books recommend treating your puppy roughly when she nips you. You may be told to grab the dog's muzzle, push down on her tongue, or even to bite her back!

Well, aggression begets aggression. Many puppies will become frantic with this type of handling and will respond by biting more, not less.

We want our family dogs to love and trust us. Any method that inspires fear will undermine the relationship between your dog and your family.

And any method that requires force cannot be safely performed by a child, so you run the risk of teaching the dog to be gentle only with people big enough and scary enough to manhandle her.

DANGER AREA

haviors belong here too. A dog consistently moving away from a child is also saying, "enough already." This is much more subtle, but still requires the parent to take immediate action.

Teaching Bite Inhibition

Teaching Liffey to be gentle with her mouth is vital. Dogs don't have hands; they use their mouths to explore the world. (Much like babies do.) We can't simply tell them, "I don't like your mouth." Instead we need to teach Liffey to use her mouth very gently on people.

It's best to gradually teach the puppy to lower the intensity and frequency of her bites. To be fair, the bites that you are complaining about probably wouldn't cause an objection from another puppy. You are missing a protective layer of fur, but Liffey doesn't realize that makes a difference until you teach her.

Begin focusing on bites that actually hurt. Once you've eliminated those, work on bites that seem a bit rough, but don't hurt (sometimes these are the teeth hitting your skin, but not clamping down). And finally, choose your family's desired level of mouthing and eliminate everything above that.

My own preference has always been to allow very gentle mouthing even into adulthood. I believe this gives the dog regular practice in being gentle; it keeps her skills sharp, so to speak. My hope is—if the terrible day ever comes that a dog of mine bites a child—the bite would be so soft that it wouldn't leave a scratch. (So far, I have been fortunate enough not to test this theory and I hope I never will. But all dogs have the potential to bite, so it is up to us to teach them to be gentle.)

To begin, the next time Liffey nips you too hard, try responding as puppies do . . . with a loud yelp. "Yipe!" Shoot for a high-pitched short sound. (Men may prefer to whistle to get a higher sound.) Most puppies will be startled and will back up when you yelp.

The first one is free. You'll yelp and then you'll play with the puppy again. If Liffey nips at you again, yelp, get up quickly, and walk away. Puppies quickly learn to inhibit the intensity of their bites so that they don't lose their playmate.

One qualifier applies here for family dogs nipping children, the dog must lose everyone. If Liffey nips Luke too hard, you should get up and leave the room with him. Plenty of dogs would be perfectly content to see the kids leave for a while so they could have a little quality time with Mom or Dad. Dogs need to understand that parents care not only about how hard they get nipped, but also how their children are treated.

Girls, Boys, and Bites

Boys are bitten twice as often as girls. As the mother of sons, I must confess this doesn't surprise me. The way you behave around a dog greatly affects the way the dog will behave.

Boys tend to be more active, abrupt, boisterous, and noisy. Dogs are excited by movement and need to be taught how to inhibit their intensity and behave appropriately when children are all revved up.

BE A TREE

Teaching children to "be a tree" is a great safety technique. Encourage the children to stand with their feet planted hip-width apart (for "strong roots"). Tell them to "fold their branches," by clasping their hands together in front of their bodies. Then they should "watch their roots grow," by looking at their feet and counting to the highest number they know.

This technique keeps the children's minds, hands, and eyes busy doing a specific task that requires no decision making, very little movement, and is not subject to interpretation. While the children are occupied with that task, the dog has time to relax and walk away.

Be A Tree
1. Plant Your Feet
2. Fold Your Arms
3. Look Down at the Ground

Girls, on the other hand, invade a dog's space too far and too often. They hug and hug and hug again. Girls are also more likely to "dress up" a dog. They need to be taught to respect the dog's wishes and to let Liffey leave tea parties on her own schedule, not theirs.

The Freeze Dance

The freeze dance is a popular preschool activity. The teacher will turn on some music and encourage the children to get all their wiggles, jiggles, and giggles out. When the music stops, all the kids must freeze in position and stay that way until the music resumes.

A modified version of the freeze dance is an effective tool for teaching kids how to be safe around dogs. First practice without your dog; you can pretend to be the dog. Have your kids dance around the living room and when you get within 3 feet of them, they must freeze in the "be a tree" position.

FASTER THAN FLUFFY?

"He would have bitten me, but I pulled away fast enough."

Nope, sorry. A dog can bite you five times in the time it takes you to pull away. It takes a dog only four hundredths of a second to bite, and a human with quick reflexes still needs a good two tenths of a second to pull away.

So if the dog snapped at you and missed, she meant to deliver a warning, not a bite.

Thank your dog for sharing that valuable information and begin looking at what kind of management and training you need to provide to eliminate the need for her to deliver any such warnings in the future. A good trainer can help.

When you move away, they can unfreeze. Practice this over and over. Take turns being the dog. When the kids are very good at becoming trees, eliminate the silly antics and have the kids do something simple like rolling a ball across the

CHILDHOOD INJURIES

Dog bites are very serious and most can be avoided with proper supervision and management. Being around a dog is nowhere near the most dangerous aspect of your children's lives.

- Every year, 4.7 million people are bitten by a dog.
- 60% of these bites are to children 12 and under
- Boys receive twice as many bites as girls.
- Boys between 5 and 9 are in the highest risk group
- 61% of dog bites happen in familiar settings—at home or a friend or relative's house
- 800,000 people (both children and adults) seek medical attention each year for dog-bite injuries.
- Each year approximately 10-20 people die from dog bites; the majority are children.

Scary stuff, huh? Here's how dog bites compare to other dangers our children face:

- Approximately 3.5 million children 14 and under get injured each year playing sports
- Sports-related injuries result in more than 775,000 children being treated in hospital emergency rooms each year
- Sports and other recreational activities account for 21% of traumatic brain injuries in U.S. kids
- Children between 5 and 14 account for 40% of all sports-related injuries.
- Every year, 900,000 to 1 million U.S. children experience nonfatal child maltreatment.
- Homicide is the fourth leading cause of death for U.S. children between 1 and 9 years of age and the fifth leading cause of death for kids between 10 and 14
- Motor vehicle crashes are the leading cause of death for children between 3 and 14
- In 2002, 130 children between 1-14 died from bike accidents, 419 died from firearms, 904 died from drowning, and 1,214 died from suffocation

We need to be concerned about safety in all environments and take steps to keep our children safe from the many dangers they face. (Statistics from Centers for Disease Control, National Highway Traffic Safety Administration, and the National SAFE KIDS Campaign.)

floor or gently tossing a beanbag to one another and then becoming a tree when the "dog" (you) approaches.

Now you are ready to add your dog. Bring Liffey into the room on a leash. Liffey, of course, has no idea that a new game is being played. She'll be very interested in your children's game, only to find that when she goes to investigate, everything stops. Hmm. By holding the leash, you can prevent Liffey from getting close enough to jump while the kids are getting into their tree poses, which would inadvertently reinforce her jumping behavior.

The wild-and-crazy learning stage of the freeze game is not safe to play with loose dogs (even your own) or unfamiliar dogs. That step was only to make the early learning stage fun for the kids while they rehearsed the tree pose over and over for muscle memory.

- When your kids are good at their tree poses, you can start having them practice them around other dogs. They will no longer act silly, of course. When your kids are around calm, leashed dogs, encourage them to practice their tree pose. Tell your kids that they should "be a tree" any time they want a dog to calm down or move away. For example,

- Whenever they get too silly and the dog gets a little wild. (This is far more effective than leaping on the couch and yelling for mom.)

- When they go to a friend's house and feel a little worried about the dog.

- When they see a loose dog in the neighborhood (even one they know).

 Sad, but true: "A child in the United States is over 100 times more likely to be killed by his/her parent or human caregiver than by a dog."
~ Karen Delise, *Fatal Dog Attacks*

Words for the Weary

Too tired to read the whole chapter? Hit the highlights!

- The majority of dog bites to children can be prevented by focusing on relationship, management, and training.

- Approximately 2.8 million children are bitten by a dog each year. Boys receive two-thirds of these bites. Sixty-one percent of dog bites to children occur in a familiar setting—at home or at a friend or relative's home.

- It's an unfair assumption to believe that "good dogs don't bite." All dogs are capable of biting in stressful situations.

- Dogs don't have hands. They use their mouths for everything so we need to teach them how to be gentle.

- Dogs will tell us when they need some help . . . if we know how to read the signals. Learn about canine body language.

- Teaching children to "be a tree" will help defuse tense or overly exciting scenarios.

- Dog bites are scary and—unfortunately—too common, but being around a dog is nowhere near the most dangerous aspect of your child's life.

Deal Breakers: Spotting Serious Behavior Issues

Sometimes a behavior problem can be so challenging that it becomes a deal breaker—a reason to get rid of your dog. These decisions are never easy.

You'll need to consider not only the safety of your children, but also the happiness and stress level of your dog. There are lots of dogs who do fine in adult-only households, but find living with kids too difficult. This is not the dog's fault, and it's not the kids' fault either. Sometimes, it's just the way it is.

I certainly want families to commit to a lifetime with their pets, but I also sincerely believe that occasionally it is in the best interest of everyone for alternate living arrangements to be made. When a dog can't live comfortably with children, the difficult decision to find him a new home can be a loving gift in disguise.

Growling Over Food or Objects

Growling to prevent others from touching food or other objects—what we trainers call resource guarding—is too often minimized. Many people say that they'll just prevent their dog from getting the things he guards. If Riley is only obsessive about pigs' ears, well, okay, problem solved. Either don't buy them or give them to him only when he's isolated.

 The tricky part is that the dog gets to decide what's valuable.

Usually dogs that engage in resource guarding have multiple passions. They can range from the common (rawhide, bones, and used Kleenex) to the more obscure (wet bathing suits, necklace beads, Styrofoam balls, and crayons).

TRAINING TO AVOID RESOURCE GUARDING

Teach your dog that having people approach when he is eating is wonderful.

Begin by hand-feeding Riley his meals. Scoop out his food and put it in a fanny-pack. Give him a piece of kibble or two whenever he pleases you. Make sure that you interact with him enough so that he can earn all of his food.

Once Riley is very attentive to you, you can begin using a food bowl. Measure his meal and divide it in thirds. Put the first third in his bowl and let him eat it. Soon he'll look up at you, then give him the next portion. When he finishes that, give him the final portion.

Parents know that they cannot account for every granola bar wrapper that their children open. Most—but by no means all—of these wrappers wind up in the garbage can.

For dogs, kids are walking food dispensers. That's one reason dogs love kids, but if Riley takes a cookie right out of Rachel's hand and then growls when she reaches to take it back, you've got a big problem.

When I was about 9, I once dropped a chocolate cake on the floor. Afraid that I would get in trouble for dropping the cake, I quickly reached down to pick it up and shoved our dog out of the way. She bit me once on the forearm, leaving a red mark that did not bleed. I did indeed get in trouble; to my surprise it was not for dropping the cake, but for trying to take it away from the dog.

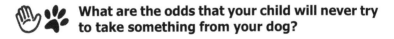 **What are the odds that your child will never try to take something from your dog?**

Even kids who have been taught not to bother a dog while he's eating still forget.

KID STUFF

Here are some things kids can do with dogs who do not resource guard.

Give your child several delicious treats. Have Rachel stand a distance away from the dog and toss the treats to him. Bit by bit, have her move closer to the dog, still tossing treats.

Once Riley loves having her toss treats to him, begin doing it when he's eating from a bowl. Have Rachel toss something better than what the dog is eating into the bowl (a great use for those PB&J crusts after lunch). Soon your dog will be delighted when your kids approach him while he's eating. (For safety's sake, no matter how well he does with your kids, don't let unfamiliar kids approach him while he's eating.)

If your dog shows any signs of guarding, contact a trainer for help. See appendix B.

A trainer friend e-mailed me this story. Her 8-year-old son, Nathan, was playing with a toy car on the floor in her office while her dog, Denver, was chewing on a bone nearby.

"He said 'Look, Denver is scared of my car'... and I looked down to see Denver chewing a bone and taking tiny moon-walking steps backwards (well they were actually moon-crawling because he was doing this while lying down).

"Nathan wasn't teasing Denver with the car, he was just pushing the car in wider and wider circles and it was moving closer and closer to Denver. Then, as I was thinking, 'Well, good thing Denver doesn't resource guard,' but before I had a chance to tell Nathan to move away, Nathan pushed the car up the bone, across Denver's paw and over the top of Denver's head . . . while making car sounds."

Nathan is just your typical kid. He wasn't trying to bother Denver while he was chewing on his bone. Kids rarely try to bother the dog; they just act like kids. Nevertheless, children need to learn to be gentle and respectful to dogs; having a dog is a wonderful opportunity to teach them to be kind to all animals. You will need to supervise them and intervene whenever your dog shows any signs of discomfort. As your kids learn this important lesson, your mind will rest a lot easier if you know that your dog isn't likely to bite to protect his chew toy when one of your kids innocently approaches.

The Ways Dogs Warn

Dogs don't behave aggressively without warning you beforehand that they're having a problem. The trick for you is to pick up on your dog's signals and respond before things escalate. Watch for any of these early warning signals: freezing, staring out of the corner of the eye, snarling (curled lip), growling, snapping (a bite that does not make contact), and, of course, biting.

Some people mistakenly believe that if a dog is growling, it means he won't bite. This is absolutely not true. Most dogs follow a pattern of escalating warnings; they start with a low-level signal and work up to more overt signals if necessary.

If you see any of these signs, talk to a positive trainer about how to keep your children and your dog safe. And remember, do not punish a dog for giving a warning! Warnings are good; they let us know that we need to make changes, now!

FIVE F'S OF STRESS

We've all heard of fight or flight, but when mammals are stressed, our behavior typically falls into one of five general categories:

Fight—threatening behaviors, which for dogs includes barking, lunging, growling, etc.

Flight—escape and avoidance behaviors

Freeze—momentary stiffness (very common in dogs)

Faint—rare in dogs, but for many people this is a common response to the sight of blood

Fooling Around—excessive activity (e.g., sniffing, jumping, pulling, or, for people, talking too much)

Excessive Fear

As discussed in chapter 2, the best family dogs are extroverts: confident and outgoing.

Many dogs, though, are worriers. Unfamiliar things frighten them, and they lack the confidence to approach and investigate. In a household with children, such dogs can become very stressed and sometimes overwhelmed by the continual influx of novel stimuli. Everywhere they turn, there's something new.

How Does He Express His Fear?

Some dogs cower, others bark and lunge, and a few will bite. In each of these cases, the dog is trying to create some space between himself and whatever is frightening him. That's what fight-or-flight is all about: creating distance from scary stuff either by moving away or trying to get the scary thing to move away..

In a family household, it's a lot easier to manage a dog who moves away from things that worry him. It's important to be sure that Riley always has an avenue for escape; don't allow him to be penned in by visitors or noisy toys.

How Quickly Does He Recover?

This may be the most important factor. Does Riley bounce back quickly or does he need a long time to adjust?

 A best-case scenario is a dog who startles at relatively few things, reacts by moving only a short distance away, and bounces back quickly.

A dog with good "bounceback" may learn to cope with the chaos of family life. Other dogs take longer to recover or may not recover at all; such dogs may appear to be "holding grudges."

TEACHING TRADES/DROP IT

Dogs love a good game of keep-away, but owners don't seem to enjoy the game as much as dogs do. Unfortunately, though, many owners inadvertently teach their dogs this delightful game. They become angry when their dog runs off with an empty yogurt cup and chase the dog in an effort to retrieve the forbidden item, which is exactly what the dog wants them to do.

Teaching your dog to relinquish items is far better and more convenient for you. It's simple to teach your dog to trade. When Riley has an unauthorized object in his mouth, offer him something he thinks is better, such as freeze-dried liver or other tasty treat. Keep a small container of treats on each level of your house so that you always have something yummy nearby.

Don't grab the item from his mouth until he is interested in the treat. If you are busy grabbing with one hand while waving a treat under his nose with the other, Riley will move away and not give up what he has.

Once he's actively sniffing the treat, try to put it in his mouth (assuming you are not seeing any of the warning signs). Most dogs will simply drop what they are holding. If he doesn't, try slipping the treat into the side of his mouth. He'll be happily surprised as it starts to dissolve on his tongue, and he'll put down the yogurt cup to consume the treat.

If the item you have taken from Riley is safe for him to have (under your supervision), give it back to him and then trade for another piece of liver! Trade at least three times before you take the item away for good. This teaches him that you are like a high-interest bank. He gets the coveted item plus a treat! What could be better?

Won't this teach him to take things just to bring them to you? It might, but what is the risk in that? There's a much higher risk in having him take things and hide under the bed to consume them. Or in having him fear you because you yell and lunge at him each time he finds a prize.

Don't yell or punish your dog for picking something up because he may become more anxious and defensive and, consequently, more likely to aggressively "defend" his prize.

Relationship, management, and training—this incorporates all three keys to living happily with your dog.

Help for Your Fearful Dog, by Nicole Wilde (Phantom Publishing, 2006), is full of suggestions for helping Riley develop confidence. Wilde is clear, though, that this is not a quick process for most shy dogs. With diligent training, you'll begin to see changes in a few months and your dog should be able to handle most situations after about 3 years. Do you have the time and energy that it will take to help a very shy dog?

How Worried is Your Dog in New Situations?

Can you distract your dog? Is Riley able to hear and respond to you? Many times dogs become so worried that they can focus only on what is scaring them. In times like this, your dog may not be in full control of his actions. He may react instinctively in ways that he would not if he felt safe.

Is This a Problem?

The behaviors I've listed below may or may not present problems, depending on their intensity. Watch your dog carefully. With good management, you can avoid some of these issues entirely. For others you will need a professional, positive trainer's help to prevent the behavior from becoming more extreme over time.

Chasing, Barking, or Growling at Movement

Many dogs have a strong "prey drive" or have been specifically bred to pursue movement. While this is a handy feature if you are herding sheep or chasing rats, such behavior  can cause problems at home. Kids are always moving. They run, ride bikes and scooters, wear rollerblades, and chase balls.

You'll need to monitor Riley's behavior to be sure that he's simply participating and not attempting to control the activity. Try calling him away. If he's just joining in the game, Riley should be able to disengage and come to you quickly. If you can't call him away, keep him away from the kids when they are playing active games and begin to work on his "come" cue in less challenging environments. Make the behavior strong before you put Riley back into a chaotic environment and expect him to listen.

Worried About Visitors

Lots of parents say they'd like their dog to be protective of their children. That's a big job for a dog. How is he supposed to know who is safe and who is dangerous?

When Uncle Jack flips Ryan upside down and tickles him, is that something Riley should stop? What about that scary guy who pulls his truck up out front and runs to the door with a box in his arms? How about those two teenagers in their band uniforms with funny hats who are soliciting donations?

Family dogs should not be encouraged to be "protective." In an emergency, most dogs will clearly recognize that something is wrong, but you want Riley to respond to your assessment of the situation, not his.

Early exposure to a wide variety of friendly strangers is your best way to avoid this problem. If Riley doesn't readily accept visitors to your home, you'll want to work with a good trainer to help him over this problem—and in the meantime, put him in another room when you have guests.

Body Sensitivities and Health Concerns

Many dogs have spots on their bodies that they do not want you to touch. For some dogs this is a lifelong concern; for example, Riley has never liked having his ears touched. But often, the problem develops over time. Arthritis and other old-age concerns can cause a dog discomfort, and he may not tolerate some things that he used to. Just like people, dogs can be more reactive when they are in pain.

NECESSARY ROUGHNESS?

Many people advocate training a dog to accept rough handling in preparation for living with a child. That sounds good in theory. Certainly it's best if your dog has no problems with being touched all over, so frequent handling is beneficial. I'll even go so far as to say that you should do some handling that is rougher than normal (but never hurtful).

I'm not convinced, however, that this will in any way increase your child's safety around your dog. Just because your dog allows you, a trusted adult, to be rough with him is no guarantee that he will allow anyone else—especially a child—to be rough. Canine learning is very context specific.

So, while I have no objection to parents employing this technique *in addition* to vigilant supervision, I caution you not to rely on any bite-prevention benefit from training your dog to accept rough handling.

If Riley has areas that he doesn't want you to touch, you can trade him treats for touches. Choose a quiet time and place, then gently offer him a treat as you touch him. It's best if you can pair the two, giving the treat at the same moment as the touch. Do not spend all of your time touching his sensitive areas. Jump around a little and include some of the areas he enjoys as well. Your goal is for Riley to learn to relax and trust you. Over time, he may begin to request some touching and massage. Most dogs learn to like it.

Take Riley for semi-annual physicals and include blood work each year for dogs seven and older. A "senior profile" records the status of all the major organs (liver, spleen, kidneys, etc.) as well many biochemistry functions such as the thyroid, pancreas, and electrolytes.

Be sure that Riley always has the option to move away from the kids and watch him closely for any signs of discomfort, which can be more subtle in dogs than people.

Tellington Touch (also known as TTouch) is a form of body-work you can perform on your dog. TTouch can help alleviate discomfort and stress. See appendix A for more information.

Fight-or-Flight Issues

We're all familiar with the phrase "fight or flight," but few of us consider how the phrase may apply to our dogs. If Riley is in an uncomfortable situation, he needs to find a way to handle it. Most dogs' first choice is to add space by "fleeing," which may simply mean moving a short distance away.

But if Riley cannot get away, he may respond with aggression, the "fight" half of the equation. Children who want to play often follow the dog around for long periods of time as the dog tries to move away. Sometimes, the kids manage to corner the dog—to their delight and the dog's frustration. This situation is a common cause of bites to young children. Parents must not only supervise, but must also intervene on behalf of the dog, to prevent fight-or-flight problems.

Barrier Frustration

It is extremely dangerous for children to approach a dog that is chained up, in a pen, or behind a fence. Dogs are social creatures and are not meant to live these ways. Many of these dogs spend their days focusing on movement that occurs just beyond their reach. In their frustration, dogs may rehearse unfortunate behavior patterns, such as barking and lunging. If Rachel wanders too close to such a dog, the dog may bite her.

Even if the dog is only in a confining environment on a short-term basis, such as being left in a car or tied out for a potty break, he may become protective of his territory and behave aggressively.

Teach your children not to approach any dog that is tied up, behind a fence, or in a parked car.

Bite Thresholds

The term "bite thresholds" refers to multiple sources of stress, that together, can create a bigger reaction.

Let's say Riley is anxious about strangers, young boys, movement, and any-one approaching his bowl. Then when you have one of your son's friends over  and his toy car zooms past his bowl, Riley's more likely to bite him as he runs by to get it than he would have been if your son had done the same thing. Four risk factors versus two.

People have "bite thresholds" too. One year, my family was traveling to the beach for a three-day weekend when we hit incredible traffic. What should have been a 3-hour drive took more than 7. We were unable to get off the highway to find a restroom for more than 2 hours, and my three sons started squabbling as a way to pass the time. After enduring this for as long as I could, I turned around and snarled, "Knock it off" at my boys. Oopsie! Apparently, we hit too many factors on my own bite threshold.

Carefully review the assessment questions in chapter 2 to help you identify situations that worry your dog. Knowing Riley's tendencies and intervening when necessary will help you to keep both him and your children safe.

Trainers Can Help

Most aggression is based in fear and anxiety, so be very careful about using punishment. Punishment will increase the dog's anxiety and could lead to more aggression instead of less. In addition, punishment may suppress the early-warning system, leaving you at risk of a stronger attack that occurs "suddenly, without warning."

Consult a trainer if your dog shows any signs of aggression such as freezing, giving a cold stare, curling the lips, growling, or snapping. Many cases of moderate aggression can be resolved through behavior modification. In more serious cases, though, you may need to find another home for your dog. Painful as that would be, wouldn't it be better to know that before a child was bitten rather than after?

Dr. Ian Dunbar's bite level chart is a standardized tool that veterinarians and trainers use to

DR. IAN DUNBAR'S BITE LEVEL ASSESSMENT

LEVEL 1. Obnoxious or aggressive behavior, but no skin-contact by teeth.

LEVEL 2. Skin-contact by teeth, but no skin-puncture. However there may be nicks (less than 1/10" deep) and slight bleeding caused by forward or lateral movement of teeth against skin, but no vertical punctures.

LEVEL 3. One to four punctures from a single bite with no puncture deeper than half the length of the dog's canine teeth. May be lacerations in a single direction, caused by victim pulling hand away, owner pulling dog away, or gravity (little dog jumps, bites, and drops to floor)

LEVEL 4. One to four punctures from a single bite with at least one puncture deeper than half the length of the dog's canine teeth. May also have deep bruising around the wound (dog held on for x seconds and bore down) or lacerations in both directions (dog held on and shook its head from side to side).

LEVEL 5. Multiple-bite incident with at least two Level 4 bites.

LEVEL 6. Flesh consumed or victim dead.

assess the severity of dog bite injuries. Dogs who deliver level 1 or 2 bites usually respond well to behavior modification. Level 3 is the big changeover in severity. Carefully consider whether—in a household with children—you can safely perform a behavior modification program with Riley if he delivers bites at level 3 or above.

Housetraining

In and of itself, housetraining doesn't sound like a deal breaker. But incomplete housetraining can start a downward spiral in a dog's life and many people who surrender their dogs to an animal shelter cite housetraining failure as a reason they are giving up their dogs.

It's common for a dog who is not housetrained to be kept in the yard with a tether or a fence, where he watches people go by each day just out of his reach. Soon Riley begins to bark at any motion that catches his eye. Then, to stop the neighbors from complaining, he's relegated to the basement, where he begins to chew the shelves and boxes out of loneliness and boredom. All the while he's getting bigger and more unruly. Eventually Riley may be taken to the shelter where, as an unhousetrained adult dog with no other training, his odds of finding a new home are considerably diminished. That's why failure to become housetrained belongs in the deal breaker category.

Effective housetraining relies on supervision, structure, management, and thorough cleanup. Treat every new dog, regardless of age, like an untrained puppy and watch him as closely as you'd watch a newly mobile toddler. Think of all the things a 15-month-old child can get into when you take your eyes off of her: she can empty all the cereal boxes out of the cabinet, climb onto the kitchen table, or gleefully rip pages out of your library books. A dog is much the same.

With kids around, you can't give Riley your total attention. For times when you simply cannot adequately supervise him, use his crate as a short-term confinement area.

Occasionally you may want to tether Riley to you using a leash. This can be effective when you and your children are reading books on the couch and you'd like to keep the dog nearby. Many people also install tethers near their front door (to help when visitors are entering) and in the family room (again, so that the dog can learn to settle down and hang out with the family in quieter times).

When you take Riley outside to go to the bathroom, reward him with a delicious treat for success. Convince him that, like OPEC, he's in control of a valuable commodity and that carefully timing his "production" can pay off handsomely for him.

Many people inadvertently teach their dog that they do not like bodily functions. This happens when we fuss at the dog for going to the bathroom inside and ignore the dog when he goes to the bathroom outside. The only information Riley receives is that you don't like him to do something that he absolutely must do, so perhaps it's in his best interest to hide behind the couch and go there. Oh dear.

If you see your dog relieving himself in the house, take him outside immediately. If he's small enough, scoop him up and carry him. Don't yell or fuss or rub his nose in it, just hustle him out to the right spot.

Be sure to reward him if he finishes up outside. Be very boring in the yard. Just stand around ignoring Riley, and when he finally goes, "wake up," give him a delicious treat, and start to play with him. This will teach him to go out and take care of business right away.

If Riley is fond of sniffing the great outdoors, be sure to provide a little extra sniffing time after he's relieved himself. If you always call him in as soon as he's finished up, he'll learn to wait longer and longer periods before going to the bathroom.

When you clean up indoor accidents, use a product designed to eradicate all traces of the mess—from a dog's point of view. Some products to consider are Anti-Icky Poo (really, that's the name!), Nature's Miracle, and Simple Solution.

Many cleaners get rid of odors that human noses can detect, but leave powerful scent markers that act as triggers for the dog to eliminate in that spot again. Do a very good job cleaning up the first time and hopefully you won't find yourself cleaning up again.

YOUR MOST IMPORTANT ROLE: ADVOCATE

Sometimes family dogs are treated more like stuffed animals than like living beings. Your job is to closely supervise the interaction between your child and your dog so they both enjoy spending time with each other. Being in the same room with them may not be sufficient; you may need to actively intervene on either your child's or dog's behalf.

A Closer Look Reveals ...

Sometimes it helps to anthropomorphize a bit—what would your dog say if she could talk? If you think she'd say, "Please stop following me everywhere," step in and redirect your child.

There are many dogs that tolerate manhandling well for long periods of time. There

This dog is moving away from the child. His body language shows tolerance, not enjoyment.

are very few dogs that enjoy it. That's a very important distinction.

By being your dog's advocate, you are also being your child's; the two go hand in hand.

Words for the Weary

Too tired to read the whole chapter? Hit the highlights!

- It takes a special dog to live with and love kids.

- Resource guarding—growling, snapping, or biting to protect an object—is one of the most dangerous behavior traits around kids.

- Even with great supervision and teaching your kids not to approach, accidents will still happen.

- Teach your dog to relinquish objects through trading, so he will learn to bring things to you instead of running off with them.

- Extremely fearful dogs find living with kids too chaotic and upsetting.

- Supervision and intervention are especially important if your dog chases, barks, or growls at movement or has anxiety about his physical space.

- Family dogs should not be encouraged to be "protective."

- Incomplete housetraining can start a downward spiral in a dog's life and is often cited as a reason for relinquishment on shelter intake forms.

Essential Equipment:
Setting Yourself Up for Success

The right tools can make any job easier, including working with your dog. Here are some items that you may want to consider using to simplify your life with your four-legged friend.

Baby Gates

Baby gates are a wonderful invention. They create giant playpens out of entire rooms. You can use a gate on a semi-permanent basis to block off stairs for safety or keep the kids out away from the workbench. But they are also

enormously handy for spur-of-the-moment uses like keeping Missy out of the kitchen on make-your-own-pizza night when toppings are flying left and right.

The energy you spend training your dog to be happy on the opposite side of the gate is time well spent. (And service technicians who visit your home will be grateful for the chance to work unimpeded by your dog's participation.)

Collars

Many dogs do fine on standard collars. Adjust the collar so that you can easily slide a few fingers between the collar and the dog's neck, but the collar should not be so loose that it can slide easily off the dog's head.

Some people are worried about their dog backing out of a collar. For them, martingale collars are a good choice. The appearance is much like a regular buckle collar, but the design allows the collar to tighten without choking the dog to prevent the dog from slipping out. (These collars are also called no-slip or limited-slip collars.)

Cordless Phones

The value of a cordless phone becomes apparent the moment your child begins crawling. You'll spend hours following closely behind. Because of the need to closely supervise your children around the dog, you need to be mobile as well, but sometimes the value of an adult conversation is so pre-

---

CRATE TRAINING

Instructions for helping your dog become accustomed to a crate are found in most dog training books and on many Internet sites, so I will just provide a few pointers.

- A crate prevents your dog from getting into things, but it does not teach her what is expected of her in the house.
- Use the crate when you cannot supervise her, but be certain that she has lots of time to be loose in the house with you providing guidance. She needs the opportunity to learn.
- Toss a treat into the open crate from time to time when your dog isn't looking. Then your dog will find that treats mysteriously appear in this wonderful location and she'll go in often to investigate.
- Stuffed Kongs or marrow bones can make the crate a very appealing place to be. Consider putting the treat into the crate and closing the door for 5 minutes before you want to crate the dog. Then she'll sit outside wishing and hoping that soon you'll let her go in.
- Don't crate your dog only when you are leaving. Use the crate for short intervals when you are home as well. You don't want the dog to believe that every time she goes in her crate that she'll be there for hours.

cious that you don't want to hang up. A cordless phone will let you do both: supervise your child and have a conversation that consists of actual sentences and real words.

Crates

Crates are a useful tool for all dog owners, but they are especially great for parents. A crate gives Missy a room of her own. Make her crate a haven with a soft blanket or dog bed inside. There are also many crate covers designed to match your décor if you want to keep the crate in a visible area.

Crates are particularly helpful if Missy is still a chewing maniac and you want to wait a while before investing in a nice bed. Be careful if you want to use something to soften the hard crate floor, though. Start with an inexpensive option such as an old sheet or a towel. If Missy chews on that item too, wait awhile before putting bedding in her crate. The crate bottom may be tough on Missy, but stomach surgery to remove swallowed bedding will be even tougher—and will make a sizable dent in your budget.

Crates are nearly irresistible for children. They want to crawl in and out of them like little doggie playhouses. Discourage this practice. You may want to let the kids have one turn when you get a brand new crate to satisfy their curiosity, but remind them that the crate belongs to the dog and is not a toy.

Tell the kids that they cannot interact with Missy when she's in her crate (nor can they play in there when she's out). Knowing that she has a place where she can go "to get away from it all" will lower her stress level—and yours.

Use the crate anytime you need to be sure that the kids and dogs are separated. A crate is also very useful when other kids come over for play dates; there's really no need for Missy to have to meet a bunch of two-year-olds in your living room. Give her a chew toy, such as a yummy treat-filled Kong (see the section on food-delivery toys later in this chapter), and let her have her solitude. She will thank you for it.

Once your dog is past the chewing stage, you might want to consider a mesh, collapsible crate. These lightweight, portable crates are great for trips to visit the grandparents. Missy will feel more comfortable in strange surroundings if she has brought her "own room" along.

Diaper Pails with Locking Lids

Trust me on this one. Most dogs think a dirty diaper is a great delicacy. If you ever have to clean up the shredded remains of a disposable diaper, you will consider it a worthy investment to get a high-quality diaper pail.

Harnesses

Harnesses are very useful for dogs with sensitive tracheas, toy breeds, or dogs prone to back problems (such as dachshunds) because they avoid putting any pressure on the dog's neck. There are two main types of body harnesses: one is great for family dogs and the other is not.

The newest style of body harness is terrific for dogs who pull. These harnesses consist of three straps, and the leash connects to a ring centered on the dog's chest. This structure takes advantage of physics and makes the dog less able to pull her owner. With one of these harnesses, you should be able to bring Missy along when you take your baby for a walk in the stroller. (The dog shown here is wearing a Sense-ible harness from Softouch Concepts.)

I recommend front-clasp harnesses for many dogs. It's important to have the harness properly fitted, so ask a trainer if you need help. It can be tricky.

The more traditional harness has at least four straps and the leash connects midway down the dog's back. This harness style increases the dog's ability to pull and is not recommended.

Head Halters

Before purchasing a head halter, consider trying one of the three-strap body harnesses. Some dogs have trouble adjusting to the feeling of head halters on their faces.

Head halters are based on the design of a horse's halter. No one is surprised that we can walk 1400 pounds of horse, yet a 45-pound dog can tip over many adults. The secret is physics. Head halters connect to the leash beneath the dog's chin rather than behind her neck like ordinary collars or most body harnesses. They prevent pulling and, when used properly, do not cause the dog pain, unlike a choke chain or prong collar. Most pet stores carry Gentle Leader or Halti head halters.

Leashes

Regular, 6-foot leashes are best for everyday activities. Most leashes are made out of nylon, which is really tough on your hands when you are working with a bouncy or powerful dog. Cotton leashes are more comfortable, but a bit harder to find. (The way you can tell the difference between nylon and cotton is the intensity of the color. If it is bright and pretty, the leash is nylon; if it is dull, it's cotton.)

Got a strong dog? Buy a leather leash. Leather is worth the extra expense when you've got a brawny dog. Besides, leather leashes get better with age. I've got one that's 16 years old that I love. Get a leash that's ½" to ¾" wide for the easiest grip.

Mats

Purchase a bath mat for each of the rooms you spend a lot of time in. You can teach Missy to lie on the mat when requested. It's much easier for a dog to learn where to be if her designated place has a floor texture that differs from that of the rest of the room. Giving her a mat will help her to understand where you want her to be.

See chapter 6 for instructions on how to teach Missy to "go to bed."

Storm Doors

Kids are notoriously bad about looking for the dog before opening a door. If your child has to open one door and then another, it will greatly diminish the odds that your dog will get the chance to take an unplanned romp through the neighborhood.

If you don't already have a storm door, think about whether your dog is a barker. Getting a door with an opaque bottom panel will prevent Missy from enlisting as a deputy on the Squirrel & Cat Alert Team (SCAT).

Tethers

Many parents find the use of tethers helpful. Some install a small ring in the baseboard somewhere in their entryway and attach a short leash to it so that they can hook the dog up when people are entering and leaving. (You'd be amazed at how many kids

PUPPY PROOFING

Making your home safe for a dog is much like child-proofing. Take a look at every room with an eye toward potential hazards. All chemicals should be safely stored out of reach for both kids and canines.

Keep in mind that dogs love to chew. Here's a list of common household items that can be hazardous for dogs if consumed: coins, earrings, electric cords, houseplants, miniblind cords, pantyhose, potpourri, remote controls, socks, small toys, and yarn.

---

will stand holding the door open, while you fuss, "Don't let the dog out!" "Huh? Oh. Oops.")

Others loop a leash around the spindles in their banister or around the leg of the couch or a bed. It's worth purchasing an extra leash for this purpose because if you always need to search for a leash, you won't use a tether.

Terry Ryan, in her book Toolbox for Remodeling Your Problem Dog (Howell, 1998), offers an ingenious portable tethering station. Purchase a large piece of plywood (she suggests twice the length of your dog). Drill two holes through the center and loop the handle of a leash down through one hole and up through the other. Then slip the length of the leash through the handle loop to secure it to the board. You have created a way to tether your dog temporarily that can be stored out of sight when not in use. You may wish to cover the top with carpet remnants to make it more cozy.

Remember to use a tether only for short periods of time and to supervise all kids around the tethered dog. It's easy for kids to accidentally rile Missy up and the restraint will increase her frustration level.

If your dog is a chewer, get plastic coated wire from the hardware store. They can help you attach a leash clip to the end and crimp it closed.

You can also tether the dog to yourself—assuming, of course, that you don't typically have preschoolers hanging on your legs like barnacles. This option can make supervision a bit easier when you are busy chopping vegetables for dinner or walking to the bus stop pushing a stroller.

Tip-Proof Bowls

Look for dog dishes with tip-proof bases. Missy's bowls will be bumped often; no child ever picks up a remote-controlled car to move it past a dog bowl or any other obstacle. Instead they crash the car into the bowl over and over until at last the vehicle turns just a smidge and can drive by. In the meantime, you may find that your kitchen floor is covered with water.

Be sure, too, to place your dog's water bowl in a low-traffic area.

Toys for Dogs

The market is blossoming with lots of new, interactive dog toys. That's great news for families because it means that you should be able to easily find a toy that will keep your dog busy.

Food-Delivery Toys

My standard, first-choice toy is a Kong. It looks like a red, rubber pinecone with a hollow center and can be found at most pet stores. These toys are great fun for dogs when  stuffed with treats. You can tailor the difficulty level to your dog's interest and ability. Some dogs get frustrated easily, so you'll want to choose things that fall out with a minimum of effort. For other dogs, you may go so far as to invert the Kong in a cup and pour water over its contents before popping it in the freezer to make a great frozen treat. I regularly stuff Kongs with apple cores, pizza crusts, and the heel of the bread loaf that none of my boys wants for his sandwich.

Some types of stuffing may adhere to carpet. If you are using something messy, consider keeping the dog off carpeted areas. Table scraps are doggie junk food, so be sure that they make up no more than 10 percent of Missy's diet.

When Missy is done extracting the goodies from her Kong, you can toss it in the dishwasher for a thorough cleaning.

There are many different kinds of food-dispensing toys. You'll be amazed at the variety. Figure out how your dog likes to play and choose toys that channel that enthusiasm. Some toys may be too easy; others may be too hard.

Two Identical Toys

When playing fetch, kids often have trouble getting a toy back from the dog. You can solve that problem by purchasing two identical toys: two tennis balls, two Frisbees, etc. When Michael throws toy #1, Missy will run to get it. As she turns and starts heading back, Michael should wave the second toy around. When she gets pretty close to him, Michael will throw toy #2. Most dogs will drop toy #1 and run off in pursuit of toy #2. Michael can simply walk over and get toy #1 so that he'll be ready to throw again upon her return.

For those retrievers who are obsessed with carrying two, three, or, in a few cases, even four balls, just increase your number to one toy more than the dog can carry, so there will always be one available for your kids to throw.

Treats

Keep small containers of high-value treats in several spots around your house. Pick something that doesn't spoil easily, like freeze-dried liver or jerky strips. These treats can be used to reward Missy when she does something you like, for trades when she picks up something that doesn't belong to her, or for spontaneous training games the kids may like to play with her.

Make sure the treats are very small (pea size is good) so that you won't be filling Missy up on junk food and you won't need to refill the container often.

Things to Use With Caution

The following items have some pros and cons that you should consider before using them with your dog.

Seatbelts for Dogs

I'm going to stir up some controversy here . . . but I think parents need to be careful about using a seatbelt for Missy if she is within Michael's reach.

Many dog bites occur because the dog cannot move away from a stressful situation. Ensure that Michael cannot spend time petting and poking Missy on each car ride.

You are going to have to decide what works best for your family as far as safe transport. A lot will depend on the size of your dog and the size of your vehicle. You need to balance safety in a crash against day-to-day safety of kids and dogs in close proximity.

Swing Sets and Baby Swings

Dogs find rapid back-and-forth motion very exciting. Add some laughing and screaming, and you've got a potentially dangerous situation on your hands. Swings are not a problem for all dogs, but many get too excited and can begin to play roughly with the children.

Two extreme examples occurred in Maryland, where two infants died when the family dog dragged them out of a baby swing. If you choose to use a swing, use a baby gate to keep Missy away from Michael. And never, ever leave your dog alone with your baby—whether he's in a baby swing or not.

Wading Pools

For most dogs, wading pools are fine. But if Missy is a water nut, she'll bound in and out of the pool with no regard for

anyone else's safety. If all Michael wants is to fill and dump a bucket of water, he may find it scary to have Missy leaping in to immerse herself.

Also, take into account that when sitting in the pool, your kids have more surface area exposed. While Missy never steps on Michael under ordinary circumstances, she may inadvertently claw his shins and thighs when playing in the pool.

Words for the Weary

Too tired to read the whole chapter? Hit the highlights!

• Keeping your eye on everything all the time is exhausting. There are tools that can help.

• Baby gates are your friends—now and in years to come.

• Teach your dog and your children to consider a crate to be "Missy's bedroom." Reserve this private spot for the dog when she (or you) needs downtime.

• Dogs think dirty diapers are delicious. Get a locking diaper pail.

• Providing your dog with lots of physical and mental exercise will pay off in better behavior.

- Put a small container of treats in various locations around the house. Then it will be easy to reward Missy for good behavior.

- Over-excitement is a common cause of problems between kids and dogs. Supervise carefully and intervene when things start getting a bit wild.

Babies and Toddlers: Coping with Cribs and Kibble

There's nothing like a new baby. They're heart-meltingly cute . . . and completely helpless. You will experience moments of total exhilaration as you get to know this new little person, but you'll also feel total exhaustion as you learn to take care of her. More likely than not, you'll worry about your ability to do anything besides basic baby care.

Adding to your worries may be your concern over how your beloved dog will adjust to the baby's arrival. For years, Barney has been your "baby," and you may worry that he'll feel neglected or jealous of the new baby. Fortunately you can do a lot to ease the transition, and most dogs adjust without any great difficulty.

Don't Get a New Dog Now

Helping your current dog adjust to the new arrival is one thing; adding a dog to your family is another.

The supervision needed for a new dog is very taxing. Your first priority will be the baby, and you will need every bit of energy you have.

 Pregnancy and infancy are not good times to get a dog . . . and definitely not a puppy!

Many people believe that they will be able to housetrain a puppy, paint the house, remodel the basement, and write a book while home on maternity leave. Not likely! Babies—and the children they become—take up so much of your time that additional projects can become burdens.

In fact, this book rattled around in my head for more than 11 years before I began. I didn't even consider writing it until my youngest child entered first grade. Before that, I had neither the time nor the energy to devote to such a large project (and this kind of project never needs to rush outside for a potty break at a moment's notice).

Unsupervised dogs act like . . . dogs. If you don't channel their energy into appropriate outlets, they'll come up with their own ideas, which will likely include chewing, barking, and creating convenient (for them) indoor potty areas.

Most parents of infants are too tired to take a new dog to training classes (not to mention the hassle of either finding childcare or bringing your baby along in a car seat). But foregoing training isn't a good idea either. Untrained, adolescent dogs wind up in shelters more often than dogs of other ages. Unfortunately they've lost their puppy cuteness and people expect mature behavior from them, but if they haven't been trained, their natural inclinations just seem annoying and rude.

BUCKLE UP: YOU'RE IN FOR A WILD RIDE

Becoming a parent is very exciting. You will experience so many new things, and your life will change in wonderful and unexpected ways. It's only fair to warn you, though, that infancy may be the easiest stage of living with kids and dogs. Never again will you have as much control over your child, your dog, and the environment.

Advance planning will help you a lot over the years. Remember to focus on the three keys to success: relationship, management, and training.

Living with kids and dogs is not always easy, but the rewards are great.

If you don't already have a dog, consider waiting to acquire one until you have enough time and energy to devote to the dog's training and supervision. Then Barney will never be blamed for transgressions that he cannot possibly understand, and you will spare yourself unnecessary stress and heartbreak.

Relationship

The actual relationship between Barney and Brianna will be minimal at first, but will grow over time. The best way to develop a bond between your dog and your baby is to make good stuff happen for Barney when

Brianna is around. Whenever Brianna appears, Barney gets a tasty treat.

Unfortunately our natural inclination can be the reverse. While the baby is awake, you are so busy attending to her needs that you sort of ignore the dog. Then when Brianna goes down for a nap, you take 20 minutes to play a game of fetch with the dog. What is Barney learning? That life is better when Brianna is not around. Oh dear.

Instead set yourself up for success. Teach Barney to find his toys so that you can tell him to hunt for one while you sit in a rocking chair holding Brianna. Put a small container of treats near her changing table so that you can reward him for staying on his mat while you change diapers. And when Brianna hits the finger-food stage, "clean up" by brushing the remainder of them onto the floor for Barney to consume as you wipe her face and fingers.

 Some children are born dog lovers.

Lots of babies like to watch dogs. They light up when their canine friends enter the room. I have worked with a number of families that have told me their children clearly adored the family dog even before the children were able to speak.

That adoration and interest is likely to increase when the child enters toddlerhood—but this is also when you may see that the feelings are not necessarily mutual. Barney may not find Brianna as charming as you do and may become worried when she starts invading his space or moving his toys. Supervise carefully and intervene often.

PREGNANCY: TIME TO PREPARE

You have 9 months to prepare and there's a lot to do, so let's get started! Do not spend all of your spare time cuddling and coddling your dog. That will just make the changes even harder.

Do you need to do some training with your dog? If so, sign up for a class. Talk to the trainer about which behaviors should receive the most attention (usually leave it, drop it, sit, and go to bed).

Please don't put this off! By the end of your pregnancy, you may be uncomfortable and not interested in attending a training class. Also, behaviors that have been practiced over time are much stronger than newly mastered skills. Your dog will be happier if he knows what you want him to do.

Will there be changes to your dog's routine? Start making those now. Put his bed where you will want it to be when the baby arrives. Start using baby gates from time to time to block him in and out of rooms. Change his walking and exercise patterns so that he doesn't expect the same routine each day. Dogs are creatures of habit; he'll need to learn to roll with the changes.

If you are concerned, ask a trainer to assess your dog for safety around children. Also look for a dogs and babies class in your area to get tips for your specific situation. The Dogs & Storks program from Family Paws is offered in most states (see appendix B).   DOGS STORKS

Management

In the baby stage, management is the most important of the three keys to success. Set yourself up for success by thinking things through ahead of time.

Coming Home for the First Time

The journey of a thousand miles begins with a single step. For you, your dog, and your baby, that step is getting you and the baby through your front door for the first time.

But you can prepare for that initial step beforehand by capitalizing on your dog's fascination with scents. Send home something from the hospital with both your scent and Brianna's. Let Barney sniff this item to his heart's content, but do not allow him to play with it as a toy. This exercise will help him to "recognize" Brianna when she comes home.

It often works well for Dad to carry in the baby, while Mom comes in and greets the dog. Just act as you usually do, come in, say hi, and then go sit on the couch. That's about as far as new moms want to walk anyway.

If your dog is a jumper (and especially if Mom had a C-section), consider having a third person help you. In these cases, it's easiest if Dad handles Barney while Mom comes in. Grandma can carry in Brianna; she'll be delighted to be asked. If you don't have a third person, tether your dog with a leash when Mom enters. You really don't want to walk through the door and then yell at Barney because he inadvertently hurt you doing his welcome-home dance.

For the first meeting, take things slow. Have Barney go over and visit with Mom first. This will give him a chance to say hello, settle down a bit, and have another opportunity to investigate Brianna's scent before meeting her. Let Barney spend as much time as he wants with Mom. When you are ready, bring Brianna over. One parent can hold the baby, while the other supervises Barney. Let him sniff her feet for a moment or two and then give him a (previously prepared) stuffed Kong or a chew bone.

Offer Barney many brief chances to sniff Brianna during calm moments over the coming hours and days. Don't be in a hurry. They have a lifetime to become friends.

The First Few Months

Time is going to be a blur over the next few months. You'll be operating largely on autopilot.

During this time, you'll be glad you taught your dog how to use challenging toys, such as Kongs. Buy several Kongs and then stuff them all once a week. Keep them in the fridge or freezer, so that you'll always have one available when you want it. Give Barney a Kong after Brianna wakes up, so he can learn to equate Brianna with "good stuff." Chewing intently on his toy, Barney will love hanging out with you as you feed, dress, change, and cuddle with Brianna.

Teach Barney the names of some of his toys. Then, when he's looking for something to do, you can encourage him to go find his snake, rope, or ball. He'll merrily go off on a hunt and will return victorious, shaking his toy in his mouth. Then, if you wish, you can play a short game of fetch with him, tossing the toy out into the hallway (or even better, down

---

INFANT FATALITIES

It's extremely uncommon for a family dog to kill a child. Most of the cases have involved babies under 2 months old. Karen Delise, in her book *Fatal Dog Attacks*, suggests that it may take 2 months for dogs to recognize children as family members.

Use extreme caution in the first few months of any child/ dog relationship—both now and later when your child is older and you add another dog to your family. Do not leave any child unattended with a dog. Learn to recognize body-language signals (see chapter 3) so you will know when to intervene. When in doubt, always err on the side of caution.

Only once have I evaluated a dog that I thought might actually kill the family's 9-day-old baby. The dog, a dachshund, was very predatory and very scary. I hope not to see another in my career.

the stairs) for him to pursue. It's a great way for Barney to expend some energy without taxing you.

Practice having Barney "go to bed" (as taught later in this chapter) when you are changing diapers. I always preferred to change diapers on the floor because there was no worry about a baby rolling off and plenty of room to maneuver. Being so close to aromatic diapers and a wiggling baby is awfully tempting for a dog. Regardless of where you choose to change Brianna, if Barney's always on the mat, you won't have to worry about him being underfoot or too closely involved in the process.

Going Mobile

As your child begins rolling, crawling, and then toddling along, her increased mobility may begin to worry Barney. Whereas before Brianna stayed where you put her, now she can get into things. She'll begin exploring behind the couch and under the coffee table, areas that once belonged only to the dog. This is when problems may begin to surface.

If your dog shows any signs of resource guarding (see chapter 4), pick up all of his toys and bones and call a trainer.

You are more likely to encounter space issues. Always give your dog an escape avenue. That sounds so obvious, but, believe me, I've been to several houses where the kids' paraphernalia littered the floor to the extent that the dog felt trapped.

TEACHING TOTS TO BE TENDER

Toddlers are fascinated by dogs, but they don't understand that dogs require gentle treatment. You need to supervise to prevent Brianna from pulling on fur, tugging tails, or poking at eyes.

Your child is not trying to hurt the dog; she's simply trying to learn about him. However, the dog needs protection from such explorations. Just as you wouldn't allow your child to poke at an infant, you also need to supervise her interactions with the dog.

Use touch-and-feel books so that Brianna can touch to her heart's content and then practice petting dogs (and stuffed animals) together. Talk about how gentle touching can make dogs happy.

Tell Brianna that things that hurt us also hurt animals. Remind her that it's not good manners to interrupt a dog while he's eating or sleeping.

 Be sure that your dog always has space so that he can move away if he chooses.

If your dog is allowed on furniture, keep fight-or-flight issues in mind. Bella, an 8-year-old beagle, bit 13-month-old Emily when she began using furniture to pull herself up. One day Bella's afternoon nap on an armchair was interrupted by the sudden appearance of Emily, who had grabbed onto the seat cushion to pull herself to a standing position.

Bella couldn't back up because the arms and back of the chair confined her. She reacted by biting Emily's face. Fortunately, she showed excellent bite inhibition, and Emily's only injury was a small red mark that faded after a few hours. Emily's mother called me immediately, and we made an appointment to meet the next day. With some changes in management and supervision—such as carefully supervising to make sure that Bella always has an escape route and using baby gates to keep Bella and Emily apart when the parents can't be right beside them—I believe this family will be able to safely manage the interactions of Emily and Bella to prevent any future incidents.

In addition to escape routes, be sure that Barney has a place that is all his own, a place where Brianna will not be allowed to go. For many dogs that will be his crate, but it can be a bed or a special corner. Clearly define the area so that you will be certain to always head Brianna off when she's waddling towards Barney's haven.

Don't allow your child to pull or lean on your dog. The only time Midas ever growled at one of my kids was when 10-month-old Justin crawled over and up her ribs with sticky fingers. I'm guessing that he hurt her, but she might have been reacting simply out of fear. In either case, I was too far away and should have been there to intervene before he crawled on her. That was my fault, not hers.

We expect more tolerant behavior out of dogs than is expected of adult members of any other species, including humans. Really. Think about it. How often do you just grab your dog to pull something out of his coat or flip up an ear to see if it needs to be cleaned?

Now imagine doing that to a cat . . . or your spouse. You'll certainly do it to your kids—for a few years—but as they age, they'll start telling you to back off a bit. Let's try to give dogs some of the same consideration.

Do You Need Help?

An active dog will still need lots of exercise. A dog walker can be a big help. There are many professional dog walkers, but you may also have a friend or neighbor who'd be willing to take Barney for a walk each day. Ask friends without dogs too. Sometimes they don't have the time or energy to own a dog, but enjoy spending time with a "borrowed dog."

HOW CAN I HELP WITH THE NEW BABY?

Friends and family will want to help when your new baby arrives.
Let them! Here's a list of ideas to get you started.

- [ ] Stuff several Kongs and put them in the freezer.
- [ ] Purchase a copy of *Living with Kids and Dogs . . . Without Losing Your Mind* for the parents and grandparents
- [ ] Watch the baby so one or both parents can walk or play with the dog.
- [ ] Walk the dog for 30 minutes.
- [ ] Scoop the yar.
- [ ] Take the dog to the groomer or vet as needed.
- [ ] Keep the dog for a weekend.
- [ ] Play fetch with the dog.
- [ ] Help arrange furniture so the dog has plenty of escape routes when the baby starts to crawl.
- [ ] Purchase a crate and train the dog to enjoy using it.
- [ ] Provide bully sticks or pig's ears so the dog can have some dedicated chewing time each day (if there are no resource-guarding issues).
- [ ] Make a conscious effort to ask about the dog, not just when the baby is born, but always. Parents may have concenrs that friends and family can help address.
- [ ] Visit www.livingwithkidsanddogs.com for more information about helping kids and dogs develop happy, healthy relationships.

If Barney likes other dogs, you can't beat the energy outlet of dogs playing together. See if you can set up play dates with neighboring dogs. If that's not possible, many places now have dog daycare facilities. One very active day at daycare may give you several days with a calm dog, a worthy investment in your sanity. Appendix A provides more information about dog daycares.

Underexercised dogs get into mischief. To be fair, it's not really mischief—it's normal dog behavior—but it may not be behavior you are used to seeing in Barney. You have options when you are bored. You can watch TV, take a bike ride, read a book, or eat chocolate chip cookies. Barney cannot just decide to go for an hour-long walk without you. Instead, he'll do what dogs do . . . chew, bark, dig, pester you for attention, or patrol the house looking for crumbs. Help him to find an appropriate outlet for his energy.

Training

Teaching Barney a few behaviors and practicing them until they are strong will be time well spent. Dogs find great comfort in knowing what is expected of them. Uncertainty makes them anxious, so take time to teach Barney what you want him to know and he'll be a happier family member.

Sit

Sit is a wonderful foundation skill. Think of all the behavior problems that could be solved simply by telling your dog to sit. If he's jumping up to look for cookies on the counter, tell him to sit. If your mother-in-law is trying to come through the front door, tell him to sit. If he's busy nudging his way into the diaper bag, tell him to sit.

Fortunately sit is also an easy skill to teach if your dog doesn't already know it. (Well, of course, he knows how to sit, but does he sit when you ask him to?)

Take a treat and hold your hand level with Barney's nose. Gently move the treat toward his nose, aiming to go straight back over his head. Basically you are invading his space. If you hold the treat just barely above his nose, he will probably fold his hind legs under as he moves out of the way of your hand.

The moment he sits, click your tongue and give him the treat. Once he is good at this, begin saying the word "sit" before you lure him into position. Soon you'll be able to get Barney to sit simply by saying "sit." Make a distinction between your physical and verbal cues. Most dogs rely on body language even when their families believe the dog understands their words. Having a verbal cue is a big help when your hands are full, as they often will be.

Go to Bed

Teaching Barney to "go to bed" or "settle" on his mat is well worth your training time. Purchase a few bath mats and put one in each of the rooms where you spend a lot of time. Having a clearly defined area, such as a mat, makes training easier for both you and Barney. He will learn faster if the flooring changes beneath his feet.

Training "go to bed" will go faster if you can pay full attention to Barney, so this is a great skill to teach before Brianna arrives. If your baby has already been born, try to do your first few training sessions when Brianna is sleeping or someone else is available to watch her so you can focus exclusively on Barney.

 Short training sessions are more fun and more fruitful.

Decide that you will only train for 5 minutes at a time. Longer training sessions can be frustrating for both of you. Make note of how far you progress in each session. They will build upon each other, and soon you will have the full behavior.

FOUR HABITS TO CHANGE BEFORE THE BABY ARRIVES

Jumping Up. For the next few years, you will be carrying some-one or something almost every time you come through the door. Practice having Barney greet you without jumping by teaching him to sit and wait for a release word.

Free Feeding. Put Barney on a regular schedule of meals. There are numerous health benefits to this, but the biggest benefit will be that Brianna will never get to taste kibble or dump the whole bowl of food into Barney's water dish.

Pawing You for Attention. If you are holding Brianna and Barney plops his paw up onto your lap with a big ker-thunk, you will be really annoyed. If Barney does this, get up and walk away. Be sure to interact with him when he sits beside you without pawing.

Drinking Out of the Toilet Bowl. Open toilets are a safety haz-ard for toddlers, not to mention unsanitary. Give Barney a water bowl and remind yourself to keep the toilet lid down.

Begin with a small bowl of treats that you can toss. Sit somewhere in the room and watch Barney. Just watch him; don't try to entice him toward the mat or tell him to go there. Any time he looks in the general direction of his mat, click your tongue and toss a treat toward the mat.

Soon, he'll be hanging out near the mat because that's where the treats arrive. At this point, begin watching his paws. When he has one paw (any paw) on the mat, click your tongue and toss a treat to him.

How's he doing? Remember, only 5 minutes per session. It might be time for a break.

When he's pretty consistent about having at least one paw on the mat, raise your criteria to two. Now you will only click your tongue when he has any two paws on the mat. Has he got that? Then let's go for three paws.

When Barney hangs out with three paws on the mat, you can begin adding your cue word. Many people like "go to bed" or "settle." Pick something easy.

Start moving around the room. Click and toss treats only when Barney has three paws on the mat, regardless of where you are. Most dogs will get bored watching you and will lie down. That's wonderful. Definitely toss treats for that. In the initial stages of training, keep your rate of re-inforcement high enough that Barney thinks moving away isn't worth it. If he just stays on his mat, good stuff keeps coming.

You may also want to use the "magic mat" concept. Each time you leave the room, toss a single treat onto the mat without letting Barney see. Then when you return to the room later, he'll find that the mat is a very reinforcing place to be. It's magic. Treats apparently grow there spontane-ously. But if you have an active toddler, the magic mat may not be a good idea. You don't want Brianna consuming Bar-ney's liver treats. Yuck.

Leave It

Ordinarily, I don't teach a separate "leave it" cue. The Name Game works just fine. However in the early years with ba-bies and toddlers, we run the risk of regularly saying Bar-ney's name with an exasperated inflection simply because there's so much stuff around for him to investigate. If you find yourself falling into that trap, develop a separate cue that means for Barney to turn away from what he is looking at.

So, we are going to teach this just like we teach the Name Game. Say "leave it" in a happy, energetic voice. When Barney turns toward you, click your tongue and give him a treat. If he does not turn toward you, get up and walk away from him.

We are conditioning a good habit. Habits are hard to break, so soon he'll look every time you call him. And in doing so, he'll look away from what he was just about to pick up.

Drop It

Oops, you didn't see Barney pick up the pacifier and now he's gleefully prancing around, looking a bit ridiculous with it sticking out of his mouth.

Use the Name Game to get Barney's attention. Then offer him a trade, a piece of liver for the pacifier. Most dogs willingly drop things when you offer them something else. Chapter 4 covers trades in greater detail.

These four cues—sit, go to bed, leave it, and drop it—will solve most of your issues.

You may also want to train your dog to recognize boundary ropes, so you can create a portable barrier wherever you go. Boundary rope training is covered in chapter 8.

Words for the Weary

Too tired to read the whole chapter? Hit the highlights!

- You have more control over the baby, the dog, and the environment in the first year than you will ever have again.

- Most dogs adjust to the new baby just fine.

- It's wise to train during your pregnancy. Doing so then will save you lots of effort and prevent many problems later.

- Help Barney think Brianna is wonderful by having good stuff happen for him when she is nearby, not when she's asleep.

- A well-exercised dog has better household manners. Be sure Barney gets plenty of outlets for his energy.

- If there's going to be a problem, you'll usually see the signs when your baby becomes more mobile, not right at the beginning.

- Always give your dog the option to move away.

Preschoolers: Someone's Always Underfoot

Children five and under, otherwise known as preschoolers, are delightful. They are smart and energetic, curious and full of information, silly and serious. They keep you on your toes—physically and mentally—as you try to stay one step ahead of them.

Relationship

Preschoolers don't have enough empathy to truly understand how to be consistently fair, kind, and gentle. They are still reaching toward those developmental milestones, so parents need to help them along the way. This means you will spend lots of time intervening when Patrick and Pixie are together.

It's important to understand that the kids are learning. When they are a bit rough or unkind, they are experimenting with cause and effect. While this is normal, it is not always safe. We need to make sure the kids develop empathy in safe and humane ways.

Modeling proper behavior is very helpful. Preschoolers like to be part of a team. Tell them, "Our family never frightens an animal. We are kind to animals." You'll be saying that for years to come, but it's an important lesson. Success will be measured in tiny snippets. Perhaps, years from now on a farm field trip, Patrick may not join the other boys in chasing a turkey because he knows that we should "never frighten an animal." Then you'll realize that he understands what you began teaching him long ago.

Learning to observe an animal's behavior and then acting appropriately is an important skill. It's also a great defense against dog bites.

Learning to be Good Friends

With young children, it helps to demonstrate what dogs enjoy and to describe what you are doing when you interact with a dog.

Buy a stuffed dog that's large enough for Patrick to cradle in his arms. Talk about what you are doing as you pet the toy dog. Then encourage Patrick to pet the toy dog too. At times you may even want to pet the toy dog roughly and say, "Look, when I tug on your puppy, she doesn't like it. She likes it better when I am gentle."

It helps to use emotional labels when describing a dog's behavior. "It looks like Pixie is tired and needs a nap," or "I think it makes Pixie a little nervous when you make that loud noise." It's hard for young children to put themselves in someone else's place. This skill takes years to develop, but with guidance, Patrick can become a kind and caring friend for Pixie.

Teaching What Dogs Enjoy

Every parent knows it's better to teach preschoolers what they should do rather than focus on what they should not do. This principle works just as well in teaching your child how to interact with dogs as with anything else you show him.

PEANUT BUTTER KISSES

Put a small smear of peanut butter on the back of your child's hand (held in a fist) and encourage your dog to lick it off. It tickles a bit. After you have done this a few times, say "kisses" before you show your dog the child's hand.

Over time, your dog will learn to gently lick children's hands when they come forward and present a fist for sniffing. It's a nice way to help kids and dogs make friends. The kids learn to wait while the dog sniffs, and the dog eagerly anticipates meeting kids in the hopes of getting some peanut butter kisses.

Always start any session between Patrick and Pixie by asking Pixie for permission. Have Patrick stand still and call Pixie over to him. It's best if Pixie approaches Patrick. That's one way a dog says,

"Yes, I would like to be with you." If Pixie does not approach, she is saying that she doesn't want to interact at this time. Keep working on relationship-building activities so that Pixie learns to enjoy spending time with Patrick.

Together, practice appropriate petting. Dogs prefer firm, slow strokes to light pats on the body; however people are more likely to pat a dog than stroke her. Help Patrick get off on the right foot by showing him how to give Pixie some good strokes instead of not-so-pleasant pats.

Remind Patrick to be careful around Pixie's face. Tell Patrick that Pixie gets worried when someone goes near her sensitive eyes and ears. Most children acknowledge that they

---

HOW ABOUT A HUG?

Dogs don't like hugs. (Think your dog likes hugs? Check for the stress signals listed in chapter 3. Once you look, you'll see them.)

Dogs can be taught to tolerate hugs and even to recognize them as a well-intentioned gesture when coming from a family member (not from anyone else). This is a learned behavior, not natural dog behavior.

Do not encourage your child to hug a dog, any dog. Feeling trapped is a common cause of dog bites.

wouldn't want someone touching their face either. Encourage Patrick to gently stroke Pixie along the side of her neck, on her chest, or along her body.

Watch other dogs and talk about what you see. "Do you think Sasha liked it when Jonathan ran over to her?" Even

very young kids can correctly identify things that make dogs nervous—when they sit in the observer's seat.

Keep in mind that habits are hard to break. If we teach Patrick the right thing from the very beginning—and supervise all of his interactions with dogs—he'll develop very strong good habits.

TOO TOLERANT?

Just because your dog tolerates what your child is doing, doesn't make it right. Here are some things families have told me that their children do with their dog. I don't think any of these are fair:

- Riding the dog
- Playing "wheelbarrow" by holding the dog's hind legs up
- Using the dog as a pillow
- Putting the dog in a stroller or carriage to be the "baby"

Teaching What Dogs Don't Enjoy

When Patrick and Pixie are together, you need to be with them. Your job is to make sure that both are having fun. It's a tough job, but you can do it. Keep a close eye on the interaction and intervene when necessary.

The best way to tell whether Pixie is enjoying something is to stop the interaction, step away, and see if she seeks it out again. That's so hard for preschoolers. Instead they pursue the dog and want constant interaction. Use distraction techniques to stop Patrick from following Pixie around.

Remember that all kids, but especially preschoolers, have a

much harder time understanding what not to do than what to do. Try to avoid saying "don't" all the time. It may take some creative phrasing, but look for ways to tell Patrick what he should do. Here are some suggestions:

- "Don't pull on Pixie's collar" can be "Use your happy voice to call Pixie."
- "Don't bother her while she's sleeping" can be "Let's get a book to read while Pixie takes a little nap."
- "Don't put your visor around her neck" can be "Could I have a turn to wear your visor? I love the bright blue color."

As you teach Patrick what Pixie enjoys, you should also take time to discuss some of the things she does not like.

People like to pat dogs on top of their heads, but dogs are not very fond of such attention. They have a blind spot up there and will usually lift their heads to watch what you are doing. This puts their teeth very close to your hand. Do you really want Patrick's hand hovering over the teeth of every dog he meets? Visit www.livingwithkidsanddogs.com to see some video clips of dogs being hugged, kissed, and patted on the head.

Dogs are not toys or dolls. In theory, this is something we all know and accept, but sometimes parents allow children to interact with tolerant dogs in dangerous ways.

Children should not pick up or carry dogs—even when the dog is young or small. Coach Patrick to have the same types of interaction that you'd let him have with an infant. "Be gentle, Patrick. She's just a little baby. Why don't you sit right here, and I'll put the baby (or puppy) in your lap? No, I can't let you hold her unless you are sitting down. That's right. Now, be very gentle, and I'll put her in your arms."

Puppies are not quite as fragile as infants, of course, but we must still treat them with gentleness and respect. It's a scary feeling to be lifted and carried by an unsteady child. It's quite common for puppies and small dogs to learn to wiggle and/or snap to be put down. That's a terrible behavior pattern to create.

Dogs are also not big fans of playing dress-up. Girls are likely to pursue Pixie to put a hat, dress, or hair bow on her. A better option is to make a few bandannas for the various roles your daughter wants Pixie to play: a shiny pink one for when she's Princess Pixie, a blue one for when she's Police-Dog Pixie, and a white one for when she's Flower-Girl Pixie. Add a Velcro closure for each bandana so that your daughter can put them on and take them off quickly. That way Pixie won't need to hold still for long.

Keep in mind that while Pixie may be quite tolerant of your daughter dressing her in bandannas, she probably will not want to participate in the same activity when your daughter has a friend over. The stress level increases exponentially.

A few final reminders for you to discuss with Patrick:

- Dogs get nervous if we stare at them.
- Dogs are faster than people, so we shouldn't run away from a dog. Be a tree instead (see chapter 3).
- If a dog has food or a bone, leave her alone.
- Let the dog approach you, rather than you approaching the dog.

Being Deliberately Unkind

Preschoolers are very emotional. They are prone to mood swings and tantrums. Sometimes, in the midst of a tantrum, Patrick may hit or kick Pixie. If he does, you must make it clear to Patrick that such actions are unacceptable.

Send Patrick to his room for a time out. When he returns and is calm again, talk to him about how his behavior af-

HALLOWEEN: A SCARY HOLIDAY

Kids love Halloween. This holiday gives them a chance to dream of what they will become, to try on different roles, and to stretch their imaginations.

But dogs don't find Halloween nearly so entertaining. Their perception is that one night, for no apparent reason, the world goes a little crazy. Children sprout antennas and wings, bodies are obscured under cloaks and gowns, and faces are painted or covered with masks. Everything they know as normal and safe changes on Halloween night. Many dogs find these changes to be quite frightening.

In 2004, the Springfield, IL, State Journal-Register included a story about a 5-year-old boy who was bitten while trick-or-treating at a friend's house. The child stepped forward to get candy, and the dog lunged and bit him severely in his face. The boy required multiple surgeries to repair the damage. The story does not report what sort of costume the child was wearing, but it seems likely that the dog, who under normal circumstances interacted appropriately with this child and others, perceived the boy as a threat under these unusual circumstances.

Since Halloween comes only once a year, it may be simpler and kinder to put Pixie in a bedroom with a stuffed chew toy rather than expect her to make sense of festivities.

fected Pixie and explain, again, that "Our family is kind to animals. We love Pixie and want her to be happy." Then have him grab some treats and invite Pixie to play one of the training games in this chapter.

Management

I'll be frank. The preschooler stage is really hard. Your kids have lots of mobility and interest in the dog, and you really need to be right there supervising and intervening. Over and over. Ad nauseum.

Never Leave a Child Alone with a Dog

This is the most common piece of advice given to parents. Reality is not nearly so clear-cut. What do you do when Patrick is watching a video, Pixie sleeping by the front door, and you need to go to the bathroom? The best thing you can do is to call Pixie to come with you or to put up a baby gate between them. Things can deteriorate so quickly when you aren't there.

Work on the Name Game with Pixie and make her love coming to you. You don't want to go get her every time you need her to move somewhere else.

Food—Mine or Yours?

Preschoolers are notoriously messy eaters, which makes them particularly attractive to dogs. Given a chance, Pixie will sit beside Patrick with her head in his lap waiting for the treats to fall. Patrick will laugh as she quickly slurps them up and resumes her adoring stance. Soon, they'll form a united front against your pursuit of healthy eating habits.

If you want Patrick to eat at least some of what is on his plate, have Pixie stay out of the kitchen while he is eating. You can do this by using baby gates, teaching her to lie on a mat (see chapter 6), or setting out boundary ropes (see chapter 8). When Patrick finishes his meal and has carried his plate to the sink (with varying degrees of success), let Pixie come eat whatever Patrick has dropped on the floor.

Don't let your kids wander around with food. When Patrick walks off with a cookie, Pixie is likely to take it right out of his hand. Dogs are scavengers, so it takes a really well-mannered dog to pass up food that appears to be offered.

Visiting children may be anxious about having Pixie near if she's likely to take food. They—or their parents—may even perceive her behavior as aggressive. It's best to regulate when and where kids can eat and to monitor Pixie's behavior during those times to prevent this problem from developing.

Training

Are you ready to train? Great. You can help Patrick train Pixie by making this enterprise lots of fun. Don't expect Pixie to respond to Patrick as readily as she does to you. Even a teen doesn't typically get the same response from his dog as his parents do unless he is very committed to working with the dog.

Make sure that you teach Pixie each new behavior and that she understands it well, before having Patrick work with her. And don't expect Pixie to obey Patrick unless you are right there supervising. Kids tend to repeat commands over and over, and dogs learn to tune them out. If you are there, you can follow up on Patrick's command and help Pixie succeed—and prevent the slight "un-training" that may be occurring.

Giving Treats

Manual dexterity is a challenge for most preschoolers; they have trouble holding a dog treat and then releasing it. Patrick may be frightened if Pixie engulfs his whole hand when she takes a treat. Even gentle tooth contact can be scary for a child. You will sometimes hear "she bit me" when Pixie did not.

It's better to find a way to avoid that concern than to have to reassure a frightened child. There are many ways to make treat delivery a bit easier and less scary for young kids.

- Drop the treats on the floor.

- Give Patrick a bowl to hold while Pixie eats a treat out of it. Fill the bowl one treat at a time.

- Hold the treat on an open palm for the dog to lick off.

TIP THE SCALES IN YOUR CHILD'S FAVOR

When training the dog, give your child very high-value treats to work with (such as freeze-dried liver, roast beef, or cheddar cheese). You, on the other hand, can use somewhat boring treats like dog food or frozen veggies.

Your dog will soon learn that it is quite rewarding to listen to your child during a training session.

- Put the treat on the back of the child's hand. Young kids often have trouble holding their hand open. Their fingers curl up and form a bowl. In this case, it may be better to teach Patrick to put out his fist (fingers down) and for you to place Pixie's treat on top of his hand.

- Have Patrick sit on the counter or kitchen table (with you standing right there, of course) and he can toss treats to Pixie. This can be a good option for bouncy dogs so that your child doesn't get bumped or frightened.

If Pixie shows any signs of resource guarding, do not have Patrick give her treats.

Name Game, Preschool Style

Teaching Pixie to turn and look when she hears her name is an important lesson; in fact, it may be the most vital behavior you teach. Sometimes just saying the dog's name is enough to divert everyone's attention for a moment and allow things to settle down. Chapter 8 includes a description of how to teach the Name Game. Make sure you can do the Name Game with Pixie before coaching Patrick in the preschool version.

The preschool version of the Name Game is somewhat simpler. When Patrick is near you, have him call Pixie in a happy voice. If she turns and looks at him, he should give her a really yummy (to her) treat. If she doesn't look, you should do something to solicit her attention—make a funny noise or tap your foot. When she looks, she should earn something that's still good, but not quite as yummy as she would have gotten had she looked when Patrick called. Patrick should deliver both the good and not-so-good treats. (Be sure to be close to Patrick. We want Pixie turning in his general direction, not only toward you.)

Pixie will learn that looking toward Patrick when he calls her is a good thing to do, and looking right away is even better because it means she'll get something really delicious. Either way she wins—and so does Patrick, because you are building a positive relationship between them.

SIMPLE, EASY, AND FAST

When training with preschoolers and dogs, "simple, easy, and fast" is the best method. This method acknowledges the short attention spans of both and prevents you, your preschooler, and your dog from feeling frustrated.

If you are having any problems, it might be beneficial to find a sitter and take a training class in the evening.

Your supervision, assistance, and knowledge are vital to enhancing the relationship between your child and your dog and increasing their enjoyment of each other.

Sit-Stay

There are lots of easy sit-stays a preschooler can do with a dog who understands the behavior. Remember, an adult teaches all new behaviors. Kids can give cues for familiar skills.

As young as 2, my sons were feeding the dog by telling him to sit-stay and then scooping food from the bag. They would then put the bowl somewhere and shout "okay" to

release the dog to hunt for the bowl. Who made sure the dog stayed? I did. I supervised to make sure everything went as planned.

Patrick can do other fun and fairly easy stays. He can tell Pixie to sit-stay and then drop a treat on the floor. You'll ensure she doesn't move until he tells her it's okay. He can tell her to sit-stay and walk a short distance away from her and then return to give her a treat. Pixie can sit-stay while Patrick rolls a ball away; then he can tell her to retrieve it.

Hansel & Gretel Trails

Give Patrick a small bowl of treats and tell him to create a trail for Pixie to follow. Keep Pixie near you while Patrick puts a treat every 2 to 4 feet. When he has laid out the entire path, have him come back and tell Pixie to sit. After she sits, he can say OK and let Pixie start eating the treat trail.

Crate Training

A preschooler should not be responsible for putting the dog in the crate and closing the door, but with supervision, he can give the cue and toss a treat inside. If you have done a good job with crate training, Pixie will be happy to go in regardless of who gives the cue. (See chapter 5 for more about crates.)

Words for the Weary

Too tired to read the whole chapter? Hit the highlights!

- This is a very tough stage, but you can do it!

- Remember that preschoolers are just beginning to develop empathy. Your job is to supervise and intervene to ensure all interactions with the dog are kind and fair.

- Stuffed dogs are good surrogate friends. Encourage your child to redirect his hugging and physical play toward his pretend dog.

- When you can't supervise, separate the kids and dog.

- Preschoolers can work with dogs under adult supervision, but do not expect dogs to listen to or respect children as they do you.

- Set up fun activities for your child and your dog to do together.

- Good habits are hard to break. Help kids learn the right ways to interact with dogs now, and they'll become lifelong animal lovers.

Elementary Schoolers: Whose Turn Is It to Feed Edzo?

Close your eyes and think of a kid and dog who are best friends. Who comes to mind? Charlie Brown and Snoopy. Little Orphan Annie and Sandy. Timmy and Lassie. When you think of a child and a dog as best friends, odds are the child is between 6 and 12 years old.

The elementary school years are a period of great emotional growth for kids. They're learning lots of new skills and encountering more social stress. Each day, they navigate uncharted waters, dealing with issues like whether Samantha will invite them to her birthday party even though Rebecca told her she shouldn't.

Dogs can provide a respite from all that stress and change. They offer constant, nonjudgmental friendship. The characteristics adults like in dogs—loyalty, empathy, comfort, and consistency—are even more precious to kids as they become more responsible and socially aware.

So elementary schoolers and dogs are a match made in heaven, right? Not necessarily. It takes a special dog to live with and love kids and an involved parent to help make the relationship rewarding for the entire family.

Relationship

A child's love for her dog is not enough to form a good relationship with that dog. Even if children have good intentions, dogs and kids can still have some pretty big misunderstandings.

I often tell people about my 8-year-old nephew Andrew, who loves dogs as much as I do. He adores his dog, Presto, a 4-year-old border collie/Lab mix. Andrew is also a daredevil. (He didn't get that trait from me!) One day, when I was sitting in Andrew's living room and Presto was chewing on a Kong toy beside me, Andrew appeared from nowhere, yelled "Presto!," leaped from the fourth stair to the floor, and somersaulted, landing next to the dog.

Some dogs would have freaked out when confronted with such a greeting. They might have shied away, snapped at, or even bitten the out-of-control kid who'd suddenly invaded their space. But not Presto. Instead of biting Andrew's face, Presto calmly looked up from his chew toy and licked Andrew's cheek.

I was so grateful that Presto thought a boy flying at him was nothing to worry about. That sort of equanimity results from temperament, not training. Presto is a great dog for kids. I told my sister (Andrew's mother) that I don't care how many cupcakes her clever dog steals from the counter, when push comes to shove, he is a fabulous dog.

 Even the most patient dog deserves some downtime.

Some kids demonstrate their love for dogs by pestering them. Jocelyn is 8 and does not live with a dog. When Jocelyn visits Andrew's house, she follows Presto from room to room, telling him what she wants him to do. "Sit, Presto. Get your toy. No, not that toy, the other one. Fetch it, boy! Fetch it, boy. Presto, go fetch it!" The maternal little girl talks nonstop to Presto, who does his best to interact with her. Eventually, though, he flees to my sister and begs for relief.

I think Presto's response is not only reasonable, it's necessary. Dogs need time with their people, but they need some downtime too. Presto is a very tolerant dog; a dog less comfortable with kids would need more help and would need it sooner. Be sure that your dog always has the opportunity to move away to a private place (such as his crate) where he can go and children are not allowed to follow.

Elementary schoolers (particularly in the upper grades) are old enough to know how to be fair to their dogs in ways that preschoolers can't comprehend. These older kids know that they need to be kind and gentle, and, most of the time, they are. However, they are not old enough to take total responsibility for a dog's care. They can't be expected to perform dog-related chores without your prompting and supervision. This is not to say that they should not have dog jobs. I'm a big believer in having kids participate as much as they are able, but you need to recognize that you will be the one to make sure those jobs are done.

In most cases, elementary schoolers are not old enough or strong enough to walk their dogs alone. Once, when my son Justin was 11, he wanted to take our dog, Gordo, for a walk. I went with them, but Justin held the leash. Everything was going fine until suddenly a cat raced out from a under a bush and into the street. Gordo enthusiastically gave chase . . . with Justin in tow. Justin was five feet into the street before I could call Gordo back. My heart stopped in that brief moment.

Once we all recovered from our shock, Justin and I talked about how he could handle that situation should it ever occur again. I told him that he should drop the leash. It would be awful to have my dog hit by a car, but it would be far, far worse to have both my dog and my son hit.

Gordo is not usually a cat chaser. He knew Justin was holding the leash, so I think he seized the opportunity for a little unauthorized fun. But that fun could have had disastrous consequences.

I see lots of bouncy dogs in the classes I teach. Management tools like front-clip harnesses and head halters can make such dogs easier for a child to control, but parents always have to be aware of potential problems. Would Edzo chase a cat? Would he pull your child toward another dog? Would he lunge enthusiastically at something and, in the process, cause Elaine to fall and possibly sustain an injury? Would he be frightened by a loud noise, such as an oncoming garbage truck or a fire engine, and bolt while your child clings to the leash for dear life?

PLEASE? JUST THIS ONCE?

Have your children ever pleaded for candy in the grocery checkout? "Please, Mom? Look, it's super-sour green apple!"

Has your dog ever nudged your elbow, insisting that he wants to be petted right now?

Do you always do as they ask? Of course not, but are you aware that by rewarding the behavior intermittently, you are strengthening it and encouraging it to continue?

Unfortunately, that's true.

Why is it that when we want to teach our children "if at first you don't succeed, try, try again," they don't seem to learn it in relation to math tests or clarinet practice? But they'll pick it up instantly in these situations. You are teaching the kids or dog that persistence is rewarded, that sometimes this behavior works. Consequently, you should expect the pleading, whining, and nudging to continue unless you change your behavior.

Plan ahead. Tell the kids before you go in the store whether or not they'll have the opportunity to earn a treat that day.

When your dog demands attention, have him perform a few obedience exercises before you play. I like "puppy pushups," which means having the dog do a sit-down-sit series a few times. Be aware of how your behavior affects that of your children and your dog, and you'll be less frustrated by these "unbreakable" bad habits.

The downside of being both a dog trainer and a mom is that I see danger everywhere.

I see a zillion potential disasters each day. Ninety-nine percent of those disasters don't actually occur, thank goodness. But the remaining 1 percent is 1 percent too many. That's why it is crucial for you to know both your child and your dog before you let the two go anywhere unsupervised.

At home, elementary schoolers will need less supervision, but you always need to keep an eye on Edzo when he's around children. Such times are teachable moments: great times to help your children learn how to behave around their dogs. These moments are more than opportunities to correct; it's far better to catch your kids doing something right than to reprimand them for doing something wrong. It's not enough to say, "Don't scare the dog." You'll also need to say something like, "Did you notice that Edzo came and sat beside you when you were reading? I think he likes to be near you when things are quiet."

There will be times when your child—no matter how wonderful she is—will be unfair or unkind to the dog. In most cases, such actions are unintentional, but you still need to talk about these incidents with your child. If it wasn't serious or recurrent, you can usually just point out what happened. "I think it scared Edzo when you were chasing him. Please don't do that."

If the offense was more serious, repeated, or intentional, you need to make it clear that such errors bring consequences. In other words, a penalty is in order. For my boys, the loss of video games is pretty drastic—certainly sufficient incentive for the culprit to make a concerted effort not to make the same mistake again . . . and the other two boys try to avoid such an error as well.

Your child isn't the only one who needs redirection. At times, you'll need to redirect the dog as well. If you see any aggression, contact a good trainer (see appendix B). More likely, you'll see what I call "sins of exuberance," e.g., dogs playing too rough with kids, dogs being too wild (barking, racing around, jumping) in the house, or puppies play-biting.

When any of those circumstances occurs, I teach the children to "be a tree" (as discussed in chapter 3). That's because if the children are still, most dogs will settle. Puppies will settle too; it just takes a little longer. If the behavior continues, it's time for a "time out." Tell Elaine to slowly walk away from the dog, and if you are in the room, you should leave as well.

Think of it from Edzo's perspective, if he loses the kid, but keeps you, how big of a penalty is it? Parents should storm out of the room, hamming it up as if they're in an indignant rage. "Who could that rude dog be? My dog has much better manners!" Edzo may follow you, just ignore him and avoid making eye contact with him. Then, after a minute or two, you can all go back in and try again.

Dogs are social. They do not want to be isolated from their families. If you are consistent with the rules, Edzo will learn how to play appropriately so as not to end the interaction.

If Edzo is really over the top, you'll probably want to give him a break in his crate. Dog-training books may tell you not to use the crate as punishment, but sometimes a nap is in order! My boys have been sent to their rooms for 15 minutes of quiet reading, and my dog has gone to his crate as well. Then I read a chapter in a novel, savoring the quiet, knowing that the mayhem will soon resume.

Management

At Home with the Family

Your elementary schooler is old enough to learn how her behavior affects the dog. Preschoolers often can't make the connection, but older kids can see that if they're running laps around the house, the dog is probably doing that too. Tell older kids that dogs reflect what's going on. If things are quiet and calm, dogs will be more settled. If things are a bit rowdy, the dog will likely be revved up too. So how do you get an acceptable level of controlled and fun interaction?

Encourage your kids to play with your dog using toys. A very long toy—like a long rope, a fleece snake, or even a squeaky toy at-tached to a lightweight leash—provides enough length so that Edzo's mouth is not

reaching toward the same spot as Elaine's hand. Children wrestling with the dog is an absolute no-no. Wrestling is a mild form of aggression, and we all get better at what we practice. Let's not have our family members practice acting aggressively toward each other. Check the training section of this chapter for suggestions of safe things your kids can do with your dog.

 To calm a dog, first calm yourself.

It's important to teach children how to calm a dog down be-cause kids often don't notice until it's too late that they've whipped the dog into a frenzy. A common reaction at this point is for the kids to leap on the couch and shout for Mom or Dad. This does nothing to settle a dog! Remind your kids that if they want the dog to calm down, they need to freeze or "be a tree."

Because kids this age, especially the 6-8 year olds, still have trouble regulating their own behavior, do not leave them completely alone with a dog. You no longer have to be in the same room with them every second, as you do with babies and preschoolers, but you do at least need to be on the same floor and be listening carefully—all the time—for any signs or sounds of trouble. If you run to the basement to unload the dryer, call the dog to come with you.

Children should never be allowed to take the dog into a room and close the door (which my younger sons would dearly love to do!). Edzo always needs the opportunity to walk away. Dogs bite most often out of fear or when they feel trapped and unable to get away. Do not allow that to happen.

Having Edzo sleep in Elaine's bedroom isn't always a good idea. If you choose to allow this practice, at least be sure that your dog doesn't have any guarding tendencies or exhibit any other aggressive behavior. I know of one mother who went in to cover her sleeping child, but could not approach the bed because the dog growled and snapped at her. Since the dog had never been possessive over the kids, she simply couldn't figure it out. It turned out that her 12-year-old son had broken a family rule and taken food to his room. The dog was guarding a beef jerky wrapper on the bed.

Food can be a problem even with dogs that don't guard their goodies. With kids, food is everywhere. There's always an empty granola bar wrapper or box of raisins tucked between the seats of my van. There are napkins that somehow don't make it into the garbage can, lunch boxes on the floor, bubble gum packages in the bedrooms, and crumbs on the kitchen chairs. Have the kids eat only in certain areas of the house and keep Edzo out while they eat, especially if one of your angels has been known to be clumsy with her broccoli. But when the kids are done, by all means, send the dog in to the dining area to clean up the crumbs your kids left behind.

Taking Your Dog Out in Public

Dogs who live with elementary schoolers frequently get to go to the bus stop, the playground, and soccer games. These excursions can be great opportunities to help the dog become comfortable with many people and different envi-

THREE STEPS FOR MEETING A DOG

It's very important to teach kids how to interact with dogs they are interested in. Childish excitement could be interpreted as a threat by inexperienced dogs.

Step #1. Ask the Owner

Teach your kids never to rush up toward a dog. Tell them to stop about 5 feet away and ask the owner, "May I pet your dog?"

Sometimes the answer will be no. Many dogs don't live with kids and are not comfortable with them. So if the dog's owner says no, that's okay.

Remind your kids that there are lots of other dogs who would love to be petted by them.

If the owner says yes, then the next step is for the children to ask the dog.

ronments. But before you take your dog to one of these events, be sure that he's controllable on leash. You may want to use a front-clip body harness or a head halter for additional control (see chapter 5 for more details). Decide how much dog training and management you are willing to do at each event. Sometimes you may want to watch the game and not the dog. If that's how you are feeling, leave Edzo at home.

Many people use choke chains or prong collars to give themselves a little more control over their dog. Since these work by causing the dog pain, they can be very risky to use, especially around children. Let's say Edzo loves kids, and he's been known to lunge toward them in glee. You take him to Elaine's soccer game wearing a prong collar. Now every time he moves toward a child, he feels pain. Child, pain, child, pain—this is not a good association for Edzo to be making.

Edzo's glee may turn into fear, anxiety, or even aggression toward children. He may begin to act out in an attempt to keep kids away because his experience has been that children nearby cause him to receive a painful "correction."

Instead you should come prepared to help Edzo succeed

Step #2. Ask the Dog – *Do Not Skip This Step!*

Tell kids that dogs don't use words but instead rely on body language. Pantomime various emotions such as anger, fear, and excitement to show the kids that they use body language too.

Have your children make a fist with the palm pointed down. Then they can slowly extend their arm for the dog to sniff their hand. Teaching the kids to curl their fingers in minimizes the risk of a dog nipping their finger.

When the dog is being given the opportunity to sniff, watch his body language.

Does he come forward with loose, waggy motions? That's definitely a yes.

Does he lean forward for a quick sniff and seem comfortable? Also a yes.

Does he turn his face away from your child's hand? Back away? Bark? Move behind the owner? Look anxious and unsettled? Growl? These are all no's.

Unfortunately some owners don't understand or respect their dog's decision and will drag the dog forward saying, "Oh, he's fine. He loves kids. You can pet him." **DON'T! Do not ever allow your children to pet a dog that does not approach them willingly.**

in his efforts to meet children. Skip his breakfast and bring wonderful treats with you. Instead of correcting him for wrong behavior, try to focus on the positive. Every time he sits, give him a tiny piece of liver. When he looks at you, give him a treat. When kids come close, tell them that Edzo is not allowed to say hi until he sits.

Ask the kids to tell Edzo to sit. (If he doesn't sit for them, tell Edzo yourself.) Then have the kids give him a treat. What you're doing is giving Edzo a chance to earn the opportunity to interact with kids, and teaching kids how to interact safely with dogs. The latter lesson can be especially valuable for kids who do not have a dog of their own.

Teach Edzo a trick or two. Kids love tricks and will likely stand back a few feet to watch the dog perform. One of my clients taught her dog to bow, but with a twist. Her cue was "Who's the queen?" and her dog would bow to her. That was a favorite bus stop trick for many years.

Be an advocate for your dog and help him to manage these stressful situations. Review the stress signals discussed in chapter 3 so you will be familiar with the ways Edzo shows he's had enough. Don't allow kids to rush up to him. Most dogs can't deal with more than three kids at a time; some prefer to meet kids one at a time. Whatever your dog's limit is, be sure to respect it. If the group is larger than Edzo is comfortable with, tell the kids they'll need to take turns visiting with him.

Dogs Don't Hug

Try not to allow children to hug your dog. Frankly, dominance displays and mating are the only times a dog will do anything approaching a hug. Most dogs

#3. Petting the Dog.

If the owner said yes and the dog said yes, the kids may pet the dog. Tell your kids that they need to be careful of a dog's sensitive eyes and ears. Most dogs don't like to be petted on top of their heads, but nearly all people pet dogs this way—it's a hardwired human behavior. There is a blind spot on top of a dog's head. If he sees your child's hand moving toward that area, the natural inclination is for him to tilt his head up and watch where the hand is going. Now your child's hand is reaching right over the dog's teeth—not a very good place for that hand to be.

Suggest that your children stroke the side of the dog's neck, rub under his chin, scratch his chest, or pet along his back. Most dogs prefer slow, gentle strokes to rapid pat-pat-patting..

can be taught that their family considers hugging to be a friendly gesture, but hugs are something dogs learn to tolerate from the people they love. Just because Edzo allows Elaine to hug him does not mean he should have to allow all her friends to do it.

Jumping Dogs

If your dog is a jumper, consider using two leashes. Hook both leashes to your dog's collar. When kids approach, drop the cheaper leash on the ground and step on it, while holding your better leash in your hands.

Standing on the extra leash prevents the dog from jumping up. As your dog gets better at sitting (because the kids are telling him to, remember?), you can begin leaving the leash on the ground without stepping on it. Eventually you won't need it at all.

If you try this using only one leash, you will need to be sure that you can keep the kids away while you lower and step on your leash. It's more challenging than it sounds, and often the kids are upon you before you know it. Better to be prepared, particularly in the early stages of training.

Using two leashes also makes it easier for kids to walk the dog, with you holding the second leash as a backup. I do this all the time with young kids, but didn't on the day Justin and I went walking with Gordo. If I had, neither of them would have wound up in the street!

The best part of all this management is that Edzo will enjoy kid-related outings. He'll love these opportunities to get liver, cheddar cheese, and roast beef. You'll also notice that you reward the dog more when kids are around simply because you'll be doing more management. Then when the kids get on the bus and it drives away, your rate of reinforcement will drop drastically. Edzo will realize that good things happen around kids, therefore kids are good! This is dog logic at its best.

With Company

Once I forgot to ask a 6-year-old visitor if he was afraid of dogs. Carlton came in my house, saw Gordo, and ran halfway up the stairs shrieking. Gordo, who loves kids, followed him up and licked his hand. The boy screamed, "He bit me!" Oh, my!

If his mother hadn't been standing right there, I wonder if she would have believed her son or me when we gave our accounting of the events. Frankly the possible outcome scares me a little. Too many people think the worst about dogs for me to blithely assume that nothing would come of it. And it's even more worrisome to consider what might have happened if Carlton had run screaming through a house near a dog who was uncomfortable with children.

So first, before any child visits, find out if she is afraid of dogs. Lots of kids are. If so, management is your best option. Put your dog in your bedroom, the kitchen, or his crate with a chew toy. In many cases, it's really not worth having the dog loose because frightened kids will do all the wrong things around dogs. Their actions aren't really wrong, of course, because they are normal human anxiety behaviors—but running, shrieking, and jumping on furniture are all pretty exciting to dogs. They'll join in what they think is a game!

If you have a frantic child on your hands, do everything in your power to settle her down. Hysteria is stressful for everyone around, including the dog. If the child cannot calm herself, get the dog and the child in separate rooms, even going out of the house if necessary. It is very rare, but some dogs' predatory drives are incited by flailing and screaming, common prey behaviors. Do not put either a child or your dog in such a situation.

If the kids are not afraid of dogs, set up a proper kid-and-canine greeting (see "Three Steps for Meeting a Dog" box). Then, after the guest has had a few minutes to visit with your dog, tell the kids to go play and give the dog a reason to stay near you. I am much more exciting to my dog when my kids have guests. I pay more attention to him, and I reward more of his good behavior. He loves to have kids over because it means good things for him, but it does not mean that he's playing with the kids the whole time.

If you are busy and don't want to focus on your dog, use management options to keep Edzo nearby. Consider giving him a stuffed Kong to chew on—if he doesn't guard treats or toys! Block access to the room you two are in with baby gates, kitchen chairs laid on their sides, or boundary ropes (as explained in the training section of this chapter). If you'll be moving from room to room, use Edzo's leash to tether him to your belt. That way you know that when five boys go running down the stairs like a herd of elephants, Edzo won't be following them and nipping at their heels.

 Turn your dog into a "party animal" by rewarding him when company comes over.

Allow the kids to interact with Edzo as much as they want—as long as you are right there to supervise. Your need to supervise will decrease somewhat as the kids and dogs get to know each other. Over time, the kids who visit often will become Edzo's friends. Give the kids treats and let them work with him. Always watch your dog for signs of stress and be sure to give him frequent breaks. I find an afternoon with five boys in the house stressful; why wouldn't my dog?

Training

I love working with elementary school kids! They are amazing trainers. They follow the instructions to the letter, and then are thrilled when the dog does what they've asked. Training strengthens the relationship between the child and the dog and is very empowering. Kids often feel like everyone is always telling them what to do; dog training gives them a chance to be in charge.

Because kids pick up new skills so much more quickly than adults, kids often find themselves coaching their parents on how to train Edzo. It's a bonus: they not only get to tell the dog what to do, but they also get to direct Mom or Dad. There aren't many opportunities like that for most kids, and they love it.

Another reason I enjoy working with children is that they very rarely use any sort of physical correction on the dog. Frustrated adults frequently want to smack the dog's muzzle when he's nipping, push on his rump to make him sit, or give a good yank when the dog looks away. Actions like these can undermine a dog's trust in his family. Modern dog-friendly training techniques do not rely on force, which makes them wonderful for families because the dog learns to listen to everyone, not just to those who can force or intimidate him.

Look for a group training class in which children are encouraged to participate. Go and observe the class to make sure it's a good match for you, your kids, and your dog.

 Kids can be great dog trainers.

A word of caution here: even though kids this age can be very good trainers, do not expect (or even want) Edzo to listen to Elaine and Ethan as well as he listens to you. The reality is that kids are still kids. They tend to give too many cues—often for things the parents don't want the dog to do anyway, like calling the dog over to the table when they are eating. "Come here, Edzo, come, come here!" Kids are also prone to giving overlapping or contradictory cues—down, sit, come, stay—when Edzo doesn't comply with the first request.

You'll need to strike the right balance for your family. Knowing your child's strengths and weaknesses will help you decide where to set the standard for obedience. At my house, I expect my dog to respond appropriately to cues given when the child is standing still near the dog and talking directly to him. This prevents the child from following the dog around, shouting cues at him.

Fun Things to Teach

Everybody trains their dog to sit, but let's face it, sitting is not flashy or fun! Kids want more excitement, so teach them interactive games. Before teaching anything else, always start with the Name Game.

Name Game

The Name Game is the foundation for attention. If your dog pays attention to you when you say his name, you'll be able to avoid or stop all sorts of misbehavior just by calling out, "Edzo!"

The rules are simple. Give Elaine a small cup with about 20 small training treats, like jerky bits, kibble, or peas. Tell her to say Edzo's name only once in a happy voice, "Edzo!" When Edzo looks at Elaine, she tosses him a treat.

This game is fun to play with more than one kid. Have the kids choose spots around the room and take turns saying the dog's name. Don't have them go in the same order all the time, because a smart dog will figure that out very quickly. You may want to orchestrate the proceedings by calling out the kids' names to let them know whose turn it is to call the dog.

If someone calls Edzo and he fails to look, everyone in the room turns their face away from the dog for 15 seconds. Before very long, Edzo will learn that he needs to look right away.

Don't fall into the habit of giving second chances. Say "Edzo" once and only once, and he'll win or lose accordingly. This fun game is a fabulous way to build the relationship between Elaine and Edzo.

Rainy Day Come

Once the Name Game is easy, it's time to teach the Rainy Day Come. Every parent knows how exasperating rainy days can be. The kids are inside, and all they can think to

---

BOOKS TO CHEW ON

Beginning Readers

- *The Great Gracie Chase* (my absolute favorite!) and the Henry and Mudge series, by Cynthia Rylant
- *Three Stories You Can Read to Your Dog,* by Sara Swann Miller (laugh out loud funny!)
- *The Rosie Stories,* by Cynthia Voight
- *Rosie: A Visiting Dog's Story* and *Shaggy, Waggy Dogs and Others,* by Stephanie Calmenson and Justin Sutcliffe,
- *The Bravest Dog Ever: The True Story of Balto,* by Donald Cook
- Police Pup series, by Jenny Dale
- *Dogs,* by Gail Gibbons
- *The Best Christmas Present of All,* by Linda Jennings
- *Harry's Visit: The Take Along Dog,* by Barbara Ann Porte

Older Readers

- *Puppy Training for Kids,* by Colleen Pelar (it's focused on puppies, but much of it applies to dogs of any age
- *The Good Dog,* by Avi
- *The Summer of Riley,* by Eve Bunting
- *My Dog, My Hero,* by Betsy Byars, Betsy Duffy, & Laurie Myers
- *Love that Dog,* by Sharon Creech (Watch out, it's sad.)
- *Because of Winn-Dixie,* by Kate DiCamillo
- *The Wreck of the Ethie,* by Hilary Hyland
- *Puppies, Dogs, & Blue Northers,* by Gary Paulsen
- *Dog Bless America: Tails from the Road,* by Jeff Selis

do is bother each other and whine about boredom. That's a good time for dog training.

Give each child a small cup of dog treats. (Make sure everyone has the same number or you'll be in for more whining!) Then tell one child to go "hide" in the kitchen. At first the child won't really hide, she'll just stand in the center of the kitchen and call the dog. While Edzo is trotting toward Elaine in the kitchen, send her brother Ethan to the powder room. After Elaine has had Edzo sit and get a treat, Ethan can call Edzo . . . and while Edzo is moving toward Ethan, Elaine will head to the living room. When it's her turn to call again (after Ethan has had Edzo sit for a treat), she'll call and Edzo will head for the kitchen only to find that Elaine is not there! While Edzo looks for Elaine, Ethan chooses a new spot.

As Edzo gets better at this game, the kids can make it more challenging by standing behind doors or sitting in unusual places. The game is over when the kids are out of treats; then everyone can head to the kitchen for a cookie break.

Hide & Seek with Toys

A variation on the Rainy Day Come is teaching the dog to find toys, not people. To begin, have Elaine hold Edzo's favorite toy and tell him to sit and stay. Then she can put the toy on the floor behind her and tell Edzo to "find it!" or "find your [ball, bone, etc.]." The dog knows where the toy is, of course, so he succeeds in quickly finding it. Give him a treat, tell him to sit-stay, and start again.

This time try "hiding" the toy just a bit more—say, in a corner. After a few repetitions, Edzo will figure out the game and will be ready for you to make it tougher by beginning to hide the toy out of his sight. Once your dog is really good at this game, you can let your kids hide things all over the house. Of course, you'll need to establish a few ground rules so that the toy is never hidden in a drawer, in Dad's shoes, or up on something your dog is not allowed on.

My kids do this with the food bowl as well. Every day, one of the kids will tell the dog to stay while he goes and hides the dish. This makes mealtime very exciting for Gordo! He loves racing around the house looking for his bowl. Some of our favorite hiding spots have been in the shower stall, behind the bathroom door, and in the basement by the washing machine. This game is a great physical and mental exercise for Gordo, and it makes the job of feeding Gordo more fun for my boys.

Hunting Kibble

Dogs have been bred to do very specific jobs, yet most of them live a life of leisure in our homes where their every need is met. Sometimes it's good to make them think a little, to put their noses and brains to good use. A very easy way to provide this sort of workout is to have them hunt for their food. You can have Edzo search for his food bowl, as mentioned in Hide & Seek, or you can skip the bowl entirely and have him search for the food itself.

The simplest and neatest way to do this is for Elaine to take a scoop of dog food and fling it into your yard. Then let Edzo out to find it. This can be the perfect game for a young guest to play with the dog because it doesn't require them to interact much. Other options are to use food-dispensing toys that require the dog to figure out how to get the food. Kongs and Buster Cubes are two good options. Have Elaine tell Edzo to sit-stay and then she can put the toy down for him.

Two-Toy Fetch and Trading

When I talk with kids about playing fetch, I hear over and over again that the dog will get the toy, but won't drop it. That's when I teach kids about trading.

The best way to teach a dog to play fetch is to buy two identical toys. Give them both to Elaine and tell her to throw toy #1. When Edzo goes to get it and starts to head back toward her, tell her to wave toy #2 at him before he can begin his coy game of keep-away. Then have her throw toy #2. Most dogs will drop toy #1 and race off after toy #2, giving Elaine an opportunity to get toy #1 and be prepared to wave it at Edzo on his return.

We do not want Elaine to reach for the toy Edzo is holding! That will only reinforce the game of keep-away and increase the possibility of an accidental bite or perceived aggressive behavior.

Gradually, she can begin waiting for Edzo to come closer before throwing the toy she has. Once he's reliably coming close, she can begin offering him a treat. If he drops the toy, she should step on it with her foot and give him a treat before reaching down for the toy. If he does not drop the toy, she should stop the game immediately. Edzo will soon learn that it's more fun to play by the rules with Elaine than it is to miss out on playing entirely. Elaine is teaching Edzo "drop it" by offering him a trade.

The rule in my house is that kids trade forever. If Gordo runs through the house with one of Brandon's stuffed animals, Brandon must trade him for it by offering a piece of kibble. Parents ask me, isn't that encouraging the dog to grab stuff that doesn't belong to him? Perhaps, but it is also teaching the dog to love having children approach him when he has something. Since resource guarding can be such a se-rious issue in a household with dogs and kids, I want kids to practice safe exchanges at all times. If I see one of the kids trying to take something from Gordo without trading for it, the cherished object goes up on a shelf for a day so that neither the dog nor my son can have it.

The trading-forever rule does not apply to adults, of course. You can teach Edzo to drop things on cue by offering him a trade and then, if the object is safe for him to have, giving it back. Giving it back is important. Dogs run and hide because they know they're not going to get the dirty sock or crumpled napkin back. But if we slow down and think about it—by offering the dog a trade, giving the sock back, trading again, giving it back, then trading one last time and putting the sock away—we have stopped a frustrating behavior pattern in its tracks. So now that Edzo knows it's safe to bring you things, he'll drop anything when you ask him to, without a trade, in the hope that this will be one of the random times you will reward him with a treat.

Tricks

Kids like to show off how smart their dog is for their friends. Here are a few fun tricks for Elaine to train Edzo: spin, bow, and rollover. All can be done with luring. For spin, have Elaine hold a treat in her right hand and tell her to put that hand level with Edzo's nose. Begin luring the dog in a circle. The first few times, give the dog the treat for going only part way around, say one third or one half of the distance. Once you can get the dog to do a complete circle, you can add a cue. My son Justin likes to use "spin" for clockwise circles and "nips" (spin spelled backward) for counterclockwise ones. Say the word, then lure the dog around. Soon the dog will learn that the cue word means you are getting ready to lure him and he'll do it in advance of the lure. Give a great big reward for that!

To teach your dog to take a bow, have Elaine hold a treat in her hand level with Edzo's nose while he is standing on all four paws. Take the treat down toward the floor slowly. Most dogs will follow the treat with their nose, but leave their hind legs straight. Give the dog the treat! Once Edzo is doing that fairly consistently, you can begin to polish it a bit by waiting for the elbows to touch the ground or having him lower his chin as well.

Kids love when dogs roll over, but this trick can be a bit more challenging to teach because it requires the dog to really trust the child. The key is to keep the treat close to the dog's body. Have the dog lie down and then look at his hips. Is he perfectly balanced? We call that the sphinx position. If so, you can lure in either direction. More often, though, the dog is leaning on one hip or the other. In that case, you want the dog to roll onto the bottom hip first.

Let's say Edzo is lying on his right hip. Take a treat beginning at his nose, move it slowly along his body, close to the left-side rib cage. This will tip him off balance onto his right side. Give him the treat. Don't try to get the whole behavior at first. Think of it as four parts: down, lie on one side, lie on the back, lie on the other side. Reward the dog for making progress along this path. As he gets better at it, increase your expectations and reward only his best efforts.

Boundary Ropes

Kids like to be near their dog, but often don't want the dog to interfere with what they are doing. To solve this problem, I taught Gordo not to cross a long purple and white rope. These ropes are great when the kids are playing a board game on the floor, when I want to keep Gordo in the room with me when other kids are visiting, or when we visit my in-laws' house and we want to keep him from going upstairs. They're more portable and adaptable than baby gates, and a lot easier for me to step over!

Get ropes that are visually distinctive to help your dog notice them. I bought mine at a hardware store; they are about ¾" in diameter and alternate purple and white coils. I have two

6-foot ropes and one 12-foot rope. These three ropes can cover almost any configuration of doorways or open areas.

To train the dog not to cross the rope, lay the rope across a doorway. Stand on one side of the rope with Edzo and offer treats for being near the rope, but not crossing it. Begin to move around more and reward your dog just for hanging out on one side of the rope with you.

Here comes the tricky part: begin stepping over the rope and rewarding Edzo for staying on the other side. Up until now, he probably thought this was a game about being near you, not about the rope on the floor. If the dog crosses the rope, act shocked and horrified! Yank the rope up from the floor, then send Edzo back across the threshold. Lay the rope back down and begin again.

I tell people to pretend that the rope will give their dog an electric shock; you want to avoid that at all costs. You should never send the dog back over the rope because then he'd be breaking the rule coming and going. This is fairly simple to teach, but you'll need to maintain the behavior. In the early stages of training, if you put a rope across a doorway, but don't stick around to supervise, Edzo may cross over and decide that the ropes really aren't relevant. Remember, consistency is important.

Shaping New Behaviors

Here's a training technique that is a little more advanced, but lots of fun to try. "Shaping" is a term from clicker training. In clicker training, a noise is used to tell the dog when he's done something right and lets him know that he's earned a treat. It can be fun for kids to use a clicker or other noise signal (such as a tongue click or a special word) to reward Edzo for interacting with an object.

Put something in the middle of the floor (a box, a soccer ball, a toy car) and click when Edzo shows interest in it. Deliver your treat right over the object. Soon you'll find Edzo interacting more and more with the object, nudging it with his nose, bumping it with his paw, stepping on or over it.

You can create a plan, such as rewarding Edzo for looking at the soccer ball, then increasing your criteria so that he must touch it with his nose, then touch it hard enough that it moves a little, until finally you get a strong nudge that rolls the ball across the floor. Or, if you prefer, you can just reward whatever Edzo does that you like. You'll capture some interesting behaviors this way.

Whichever you do, be sure to use a clicker or click your tongue to help the dog understand what you are rewarding. Click as soon as you see something you like, then give the dog a treat. Sometimes it helps to think of it like a camera, that you are taking a picture of what the dog did right, capturing a moment.

Words for the Weary

Too tired to read the whole chapter? Hit the highlights!

- The elementary school years are chaotic, eventful, and fun.

- Dogs give children wonderful gifts of friendship, loyalty, and companionship. Encourage your children to develop a relationship built on trust and cooperation with your dog.

- Teach your kids to see that their activity level affects the dog's activity level.

- When children other than your own are around, increase your supervision and management to prevent problems.

- Set your dog up for success by including him on family outings and bringing treats to strengthen good behavior.

- Teach your kids three steps for meeting an unfamiliar dog: ask the owner, ask the dog, and pet the dog.

- Kids this age are great dog trainers. Encourage them to teach Edzo new behaviors.

Teenagers:
As If Hormones Weren't Enough

The finish line is in sight! Statistically your children's risk of being bitten by a dog drops dramatically in the teen years. Teens are becoming aware of the ways their behavior affects others, so they can defuse most stressful situations without your assistance. (Well, at least stressful situations with dogs. You and he may still have a few tense moments ahead.)

By now, Tyler is old enough to be responsible for Taffy's training and upkeep, but does he have time? Teens are busy people who see a dog as part of their at-home lives—someone they are happy to see when they are home (which may be rare, especially once they get their drivers' licenses!), but don't really think about or miss when they are out. That's okay. Distancing themselves from the family is a normal part of growing up.

Keep in mind that it's easier for a teen to leave than to be left. While it may appear at times that Tyler doesn't really care much about Taffy, that does not mean that he wouldn't be hurt if you decided to give her up.

Relationship

For most teens, their dog is a small part of their daily life, but still someone they rely on for emotional support. Just as she did in the elementary school years, Taffy  can provide a sympathetic ear to a teen who's navigating an

---

SHOULD WE GET A DOG NOW?

Carefully consider whether you want to adopt a dog when your child is a teen. You are making a 10-15 year commitment. Think about how your life will change as an "empty nester." Pick a dog that suits your long-term plans.

The summer I turned 16, I got a puppy. I was thrilled. I took Lucky on long walks and to training classes. (We were terrible!) I petted her and played with her every day for 2 years—and then I went to college.

I still enjoyed Lucky when I went home for vacations, but she never again felt like "my" dog. When I graduated from college and was ready for a dog, did I call my mom and ask for Lucky? Nope. I got a different dog.

Lucky and I lived together for 2 years. She lived with my mother for 14. So, you tell me, whose dog was Lucky?

---

increasingly complex life. She'll never betray a confidence or care about a social gaffe.

This canine bonding is more important than it sounds. Home needs to be a place teens can feel safe and loved unconditionally at a time when the world and their peers seem to be constantly judging them. Taffy is part of the bedrock that home provides.

While Tyler may seem indifferent toward Taffy at times, he might simply be reacting to your presence. When you are not around, he may be much more affectionate and interactive with Taffy. It's not cool to gush over your dog in front of people, but behind closed doors, anything goes.

In all likelihood, Tyler is too busy to take full responsibility for Taffy's care. He has after-school practices to attend, research papers to write, and parties to go to. He's juggling a busy calendar. On days when Tyler needs to take care of Taffy and you won't be there to remind him (or you don't want to be accused of nagging), have him add her to his agenda book or PDA so that he doesn't forget.

Nor is Tyler ready to take on the costs of owning a dog. Even if he has a job, the miscellaneous costs add up quickly. Owning a pet must always be a family commitment with the ultimate responsibility falling on the parents.

Management

When Taffy is at home with your family, you won't have to worry much about management. Your general family guidelines about always letting the dog walk away and prohibiting rough play will suffice. However, when friends come over, you'll still need to watch carefully.

 Teenage boys remind me of a pack of puppies.

Teens are very susceptible to "pack behavior." When two or more teens are together, they are likely to be significantly louder and more physical than when alone—especially the boys! They're always roughhousing with each other, swapping punches, and trading insults. If you have only one child, this new and disruptive behavior may worry Taffy.

In theory, Tyler should be looking out for Taffy's best interests when his friends are over—but in reality, he is not likely to be. Instead he'll probably be absorbed in interacting with his friends and a bit oblivious to her possible discomfort. You need be aware of what is going on. Have Taffy meet each

guest upon arrival and then take her with you to a quieter part of the house.

Don't make a habit of asking Tyler to feed or walk Taffy while he has a group of friends over. Taffy will likely be short-changed. However, if he or one of his friends seems a bit down, bored, or apathetic, suggest that they take

Taffy on to a favorite park or on a long walk. The fresh air and exercise will benefit them all and will help the teens focus outward and less on their own problems.

It's also easier for many people to talk about a problem while they are doing something unrelated. By suggesting that Tyler and his friend take Taffy for a walk "because she really needs to get out," you may be providing them the chance to have a more in-depth conversation than they would have had otherwise.

Training

For some teens, taking a dog to training class can be a chance to excel in a low-pressure environment. One of my favorite clients was 13-year-old Sarah and Coconut, the very shy Pomeranian she adopted. For months, Sarah slowly and carefully helped Coconut feel secure and grow more confident. During that time, I saw similar changes in

RISKY BUSINESS

Because brain maturation is a slow process, teens aren't always good at recognizing risks or consequences of their behavior. While most teens would never endanger or abuse an animal, a few think it is funny to give a dog alcohol or drugs, to taunt a dog, or to temporarily inhibit a dog's movement (e.g., by tying a dog's hind legs together). These activities are more likely to occur in a group setting with participants egging each other on.

Remind your children they have a moral imperative to protect those who cannot protect themselves. Make certain your teen recognizes the seriousness of this behavior. If necessary, seek professional assistance. Cruelty to animals is often one step in an escalating series of violent actions..

Sarah. Because she needed to be Coconut's advocate, she became more comfortable expressing her opinions, suggesting changes, and raising new ideas. Both Sarah and Coconut blossomed in those months. Sarah learned things that will take her far beyond dog class.

If Taffy needs basic obedience, sign her up for a class and ask Tyler to train her. If her foundation skills are good, you may want to consider a just-for-fun class, like agility, rally-o, freestyle, nosework, or flyball.

To find these types of classes in your area, contact local dog trainers and check your community recreation guides, YMCAs, or 4-H clubs. Here in a nutshell are descriptions of some of these activities.

Agility

Agility is a canine obstacle course. Tyler will teach Taffy how to jump through a tire, run through a tunnel, and walk across a teeter-totter among other things. As they get better, they will be timed while running the course.

Agility is a great energy outlet for busy, bright dogs, but it can also be a nice confidence builder for more tentative souls. Your shy dog can learn to trust you and herself more as she tries new things and discovers she can succeed. Agility provides a great mind-body connection for dogs.

Nose Work

Dogs have an incredible ability to smell and they love learning nose work. Now many communities offter training classes for beginners. In nose work sessions, the dog is tasked to find a specific odor and will be rewarded for a successful search. Your teen and dog will love going to nose work class together.

Rally Obedience

Rally obedience—or rally-o—takes traditional obedience cues, such as sit, stay, heel, and come, and combines them in various forms to form challenging, multistep courses. The combination of speed and variety keeps this canine sport interesting. If Tyler and Taffy sign up for rally-o, watch as their communication blossoms and their heeling skills become incredibly strong.

DRIVING WITH A DOG

When your teen gets a driver's license, be sure to include some instruction about safe driving with a canine passenger. Ideally, the dog will be safely restrained in a seatbelt or crate in the back of the car (but not if she'll be within poking distance of a young child).

Make certain that the dog cannot physically interfere with your child while he's driving. An unexpected "pet me" nudge could be dangerous for a new driver.

Also remind your teen that dogs are very sensitive to heat and cannot be left in a car, even with the windows ajar, on a 70-degree day for more than 5 minutes. (On hotter days, the safe period is even shorter.) This is enough time for your teen to grab a soda and a candy bar from a convenience store, but is not enough to order and eat lunch in a fast food restaurant.

Freestyle

Freestyle combines basic obedience and trick training with music to develop a choreographed routine. Freestyle is all about fun, individuality, and showing off the strong relationship between the dog and owner.

Now, before you start saying, "But I don't dance," let me explain that the emphasis in freestyle is on the dog. You do not have to be a dancer to enjoy a freestyle class. Each routine is choreographed to show off Taffy's strengths. You can serve as just a backdrop if you desire.

Flyball

Is Tyler competitive? Is Taffy ball-obsessed? If so, flyball may be the sport for both of them. In flyball, a relay team of four dogs jumps over four hurdles, retrieves a ball, and jumps back over the hurdles so the next dog can begin. Fast teams can run all four dogs in less than 30 seconds!

Tricks

If none of the organized dog sports catches your teen's fancy, consider purchasing a book or video about trick training. Working on tricks can be much more rewarding than doing traditional obedience, but I'll let you in on a secret: the training techniques are the same! The only difference is that people don't get stressed when their dog has difficulty learning to commando crawl across the floor like they would if she had trouble with a down-stay.

When you let go of the stress, training becomes fun and your lines of communication develop naturally. You start to see your dog's behavior a bit more objectively, recognizing stress or confusion instead of assuming her behavior is born out of stubbornness. And people love to watch dogs do tricks, so it's rewarding to show others what you've been working on. Ask Tyler to develop three new tricks to show off at the next family reunion.

My favorite trick videos are the "Bow Wow" series by Sherri Lippman and Virginia Broitman. More information about these videos is available in appendix B.

Unscheduled, Unstructured Fun

The kind of training Tyler is most likely to do will be spontaneous. He may train Taffy to be a goalie in backyard soccer matches or teach her to retrieve a Frisbee or ball. They may hike, swim, or camp together. Or he may encourage her to just hang out with him while he watches a movie or plays a video game. Keep a small basket with her brush and a few plastic bags (to dispose of the clumps of hair) near the TV. Brushing Taffy is a good way for Tyler to stay connected with her and it will help him to relax as well. Taffy's role through these years is to provide supportive companionship, something at which most dogs excel.

Words for the Weary

Too tired to read the whole chapter? Hit the highlights!

- Though they may not always show it, teens love and need their dogs just as much now as they did when they were younger.

- Teens are more mature and are capable of caring for a dog, but they probably don't have time to assume full responsibility for dog care, and they certainly don't have the resources to assume financial responsibility for the dog.

- If you are considering adding a dog to your family when your youngest child is a teen, carefully consider what your "empty nest" goals are. Choose a dog that will fit into your lifestyle when the kids are gone.

- Watch your dog around groups of teens. They're a boisterous bunch and can be worrisome for dogs.

- Do not allow any roughhousing with the dog. And if Taffy is anxious, do not allow any roughhousing in her presence.

Saying Goodbye:
Life Without Your Dog

The sad reality is that sooner or later, your family will deal with the loss of your dog. Your dog may die of illness or old age, or you may find that, because of behavioral concerns, you need to find your dog another home or make the extremely difficult decision to euthanize your dog if he cannot be safely and responsibly rehomed.

In any case, you will find yourself having difficult discussions with your children. We all want to spare our children pain, so it's worth spending a little time now thinking about how you want to handle this situation when the time comes.

 **Dogs' lives are too short. Their only fault, really.
~ Agnes Sligh Turnbull**

When Your Dog Dies

It's very important to recognize that your children have deep emotions about your dog. They often have a stronger connection with their pet than with members of the extended family.

Parents may find it upsetting to see that their children are sometimes more heart-broken when their dog dies than

 when their grandma did. But this emotional intensity is normal and natural. After all, the dog was part of their day-to-day lives. He gleefully met them at the door each day after school, joined forces with them in under-the-table vegetable "sharing," and curled up beside them

while they watched TV. While they sincerely loved Grandma, they probably didn't see her every day. Her absence will be felt most at birthdays, holidays, and other times when the family gathers.

Do not minimize your child's emotions by saying such things as "It's only a dog" or "We can get a new dog." Your dog was your child's friend, and she's entitled to feel sad for a while. Feeling sad is a normal part of grieving. Your child needs to go through the process in order to face the sad truth, and learn to deal with it. You can help your child get through the process, but ignoring it or making light of it can make things worse. Studies have shown that children sometimes believe, based on their parents' blasé reaction to the pet's death, that this is how their parents would respond if the child died. This is not how we want our children to feel.

Telling Your Child What Happened

Be careful with your words. Children are very literal and can find it scary to hear that Fritz was "put to sleep." It opens up unsettling images of naps that don't end. Children can develop a fear of falling asleep, afraid they won't wake up again. (Quiet time when the children are sleeping is such a precious commodity for parents; let's not make it scary!)

Tell the truth in words that your child can understand. Be aware that hedging usually backfires. Sooner or later you'll be caught by a question that you are not prepared for.

It is very dangerous to tell an easy lie to an older child. Fritz did not run away. If you tell your child that he did, she will be looking for the dog forever—on every street corner, at each ball field, far beyond his reasonable lifespan. Your child may also resent you for not looking harder for Fritz. Why aren't you putting up posters? Visiting the local shelters? Asking neighbors to help you look? If your child thinks you don't care enough to look for your lost dog, she could even begin to feel that dogs are disposable.

There is also no mythical farm where all dogs run free. Much as some of us would like that to be true, it isn't and it opens up a lot of questions about where the farm is and why can't you go visit Fritz on the farm?

The best approach is to answer your child's questions honestly, offering only as much information as she is ready to hear. Ask your child questions to see what she's thinking and feeling.

Some of what you say will depend on your personal beliefs. Do dogs go to heaven? This

BOOKS TO CHEW ON

- *Dog Heaven,* by Cynthia Rylant
- *A Dog Like Jack,* by DyAnne DiSalvo-Ryan
- *Saying Goodbye to Lulu,* by Connie Demas & Ard Hoyt
- *Love That Dog,* by Sharon Creech
- *A Special Place for Charlee: A Child's Companion through Pet Loss,* by Debby Morehead
- *When a Pet Dies,* by Fred Rogers
- *Remembering Rafferty,* by Joy Johnson
- *Jasper's Day,* by Marjorie Blain Parker

brings to mind a famous quote by Will Rogers: "If there are no dogs in Heaven, then when I die I want to go where they went." Decide what you are comfortable with and tell that to your children. Children accept answers that are given with authority.

Try telling your children something like this: Fritz was old and ill. Even though we all loved him very much, he was not able to get better. His body was too sick. So we took him to the doctor and asked the doctor to give Fritz some medicine that would help him be more comfortable while his body was failing. Mom stayed with him for a while until Fritz died, and now Fritz is running around in heaven doing all the things he loved to do when he wasn't so old and sick.

The tricky part is to say that and nothing more unless the child asks for more details. Listen carefully to your child's questions and answer only what she asked.

Be sure to let your children's teachers and daycare providers know so that they can be alert for any changes in behavior.

Different Ages, Different Emotions

Kids deal with things in their own ways. Some kids will be angry and confrontational, but won't ever admit to being sad. Others will be weepy and will want to talk about Fritz all the time when you just want to move on. Some will hide their feelings and insist that they are fine.

Check in with all of your kids each day to ask how they are coping. It's easy to focus on the child who was the biggest dog lover, but she is not the only one going through the emotional wringer.  Her brother who never spent a lot of time with Fritz, but still ruffled his fur every day when he came home from school will be missing the dog too, as will her sister who liked to stroke Fritz's soft ears while watching TV. Each child had a unique relationship with Fritz and will be mourning in an individual way.

Be ready to talk about what happened over and over. When a friend's dog died, I offered to loan her my kids. She said, "Because they could distract me?" "Nope," I answered, "because they'll make you tell the story over and over until finally you'll be able talk about Sierra without crying." It can be extremely painful, but effective, therapy.

Kids may also look for something good in a sad situation. At 7 years old, one of my sons said, "I'm glad Midas died. Now we can get a black dog." Ouch! I had to remind myself that he was just trying to process what had happened and was looking for a silver lining from a kid's egocentric point of view.

When Your Dog Cannot Stay in Your Home

A much tougher situation occurs when you decide that your dog needs a new home. Often this is because, for one reason or another, your dog is not comfortable living with kids.

How do you explain that to your kids in a politically correct way? Kids really think the world revolves around them, so you need to be extremely careful that they don't wind up blaming themselves that Fritz had to go. It's a very touchy subject.

It's usually best to talk about what Fritz needed, without going into why he couldn't get it in your home. You might say something like, "Fritz needed a home where he didn't feel like he needed to growl about garbage" or "Fritz needed a family that could give him lots and lots of exercise."

Older kids will figure out the flip side of these statements—that you and your family cannot provide the home Fritz needs—but you should try very hard not to say them. Words are sometimes hard to forget. Instead, remind the children that the whole family loves Fritz very much and wants the best for him. Assure them that, while they will always love Fritz and he will always love them, there is a wonderful family looking for a dog just like Fritz and he'll be well taken care of. Or you could say that a rescue group is helping to find Fritz a home "where he can . . . [whatever]."

If at all possible, give your children the opportunity to say goodbye before Fritz goes. It will be difficult, but doing so will help them to face the painful reality a bit better.

"ADOPTION" NOT AN OPTION?

Carefully consider whether you want to tell your child that Fritz was "adopted" by another family. Children are familiar with that term and believe in its permanence.

The problem comes up when we let one of our family members be adopted out of our family. Some children will wonder, "Could that happen to me?"

Reserve the term for when a child or dog is adopted into a family, but say something else if you need to find a new home for your dog.

Ways to Say Goodbye

We teach a class for anxious dogs, and I often tell the students that we cannot eliminate stress from their dogs' lives. All we can do is give them the tools to deal with stress. Similarly, your family needs to find a way to say goodbye to your dog. These goodbye rituals will help your children process their emotions and will give them a purpose, something to do.

Here are a few ideas that may help you get started:

• Create a photo album of pictures of Fritz and the children. Include drawings your children have made as well.

• Make a stepping stone for your garden with the dog's name (and possibly paw prints) on it. Some people also embed their dog's ID tag on the stone. Your kids might like to put their handprints (or footprints) on as well.

• Save something belonging to the dog. You can put a dog toy on a shelf and tell the kids that we are saving Fritz's favorite squeaky toy because it reminds us of how he used to race around squeak-squeak-squeaking all the time.

• Plant a tree or a bush in his honor.

• Some older kids would be willing to donate the dog's bedding, toys, and leash to the local animal shelter "because we want another family to have a great dog like Fritz."

• Bury your dog (if your local ordinances allow) or cremate him and spread his ashes in a special place.

There's no perfect way to say goodbye, and nothing will make doing so easy.

You need to think about what will help your kids the most and try to provide that. There'll be good days and bad days, but bit by bit the pain will ease. The love and happy memories will remain.

When to Get Another Dog

And now we are right back where we started . . . should we get a dog? All the questions you considered in chapter 2 are relevant again.

One question becomes more pertinent with each passing year: do you want a dog? Teens have busy lives and often don't have time to provide all the care a dog requires. Soon enough, they'll fly the coop, leaving Lucky home to spend the next decade with you. Choose a dog that suits your lifestyle because you'll be spending a lot of time together.

Getting a Dog When Your Dog is Geriatric

So, you don't ever want to come home to an empty house? Then you may want to get another dog before your dog dies. As I once (successfully) pleaded to my mother, it's a "companion dog," not a "replacement dog."

Consider whether this is fair to your current dog. Does he have the energy and resilience to deal with a new dog in  the house? Will the new dog give him a new lease on life or just irritate him in his dotage? If your dog has health issues, such as arthritis, ask your veterinarian if a new dog would put too much strain on your dog's health. Health issues don't necessary rule out another canine addition to the family.

Perhaps an adult dog might be a better fit than a rambunctious puppy?

A professional dog trainer can also help you assess a dog's temperament to see if it would be a good fit for your family—both canine and human.

Getting a Dog After Your Dog Dies

Consider waiting awhile. The whole family may need a little time to grieve and adjust.

It's tempting to rush out and get another dog to fill that gaping hole in your hearts. Just keep in mind, the new dog isn't your beloved pet. He won't measure up to the standard that Fritz set. You'll be continually reminded of Fritz each time Lucky does something differently.

Bonding with a new dog can be particularly challenging when you get another dog of the same breed. Lucky's looks may be reminiscent of Fritz, but his behavior is not. And to be fair, Fritz had a lot of really trying moments over the years, but if he was a senior when he died, those moments were so long ago that you may have forgotten the bad and remember only the good.

When you are ready to open your home and your hearts to another dog, tell yourself that you are only going to begin looking, that you aren't planning to get a dog yet. Do your research. Don't feel rushed.

Then one day, a sweet face will capture your heart and you will be unable to imagine your home without that dog. That's the best time to get another dog.

Words for the Weary

Too tired to read the whole chapter? Hit the highlights!

- As much as we would love to, we cannot shield our children from death, and often the death of a pet is their first encounter with it.

- Your children will have very deep emotions about your dog . . . and they may not be able to articulate them.

- Do not minimize your child's emotional response or tell them that they should feel differently than they do.

- Be honest with your children, but don't overwhelm them with detailed information. Answer the questions they ask, and ask them questions in return.

- It is very common for children to blame themselves. Choose your words carefully, especially if you could not keep Fritz because of behavioral concerns.

- Help your children to say goodbye. Rituals ease pain and promote discussion and healing.

- Carefully consider the best time to add another dog to your life. Try to resist the urge to run out and get another dog right away.

Photo Album:
What a Closer Look Reveals

We all love to see cute pictures of kids with dogs. The problem is that sometimes what appears at first glance to be adorable is actually an uncomfortable—or even dangerous—moment.

The more you learn about body language—both human and canine—the better you'll be able to help your kids and dogs develop a strong, loving relationship based on trust. (See pages 36 and 37 for some common canine stress signals.) Photos are a great way to get started because they capture a single moment and freeze it for closer inspection.

While gathering photos for this book, I looked through thousands of pictures of kids and dogs. Some of them warmed my heart, but others chilled me to the bone. This appendix includes a random assortment of photos with some of my thoughts about them.

Because our species are so different, there are many opportunities for miscommunication between kids and dogs, but an even bigger problem is that the supervising adult sometimes looks only at the child's intentions and not at the dog's reaction. In these cases, an adult will condone or even encourage interactions that make a dog uncomfortable, simply because the child had good intentions.

It's easy to look at pictures and wonder what the parents were thinking by allowing that interaction to occur. In most of these photos, I imagine the parents had no worries at all.

Ignorance can be bliss. Once you become aware of the signals, they're hard to ignore. When understand body language, you become aware of just how challenging it is to truly *supervise* kids and dogs. But it's worth it!

Knowing what to look for and when to intervene is the challenge.

Happy dogs have loose, playful postures. They have relaxed faces.

Stressed dogs have stiff, tense bodies. Their mouths are usually closed.

Feeling Squished = Feeling Sad

Space is really important to dogs. The two top photos were taken only seconds apart, but the dog's emotional state is quite different in each. In the first, his mouth is closed and he's showing tolerance. When the boys give him just a bit more space, he is "smiling" and more relaxed.

These uncomfortable moments are common—especially in staged photos. I'm sure the dog in the photo on the bottom right loves those kids, but in this moment, she's more stressed than the dog sitting beside the girl in the photo on the left.

Dogs and humans alike, we all like to have a little breathing room.

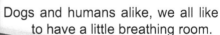

How 'Bout a Great, Big Hug?

People enjoy hugs; most dogs do not. **Can you find the least stressed dog on these two pages?** Look past the big smiles on the faces of these adorable children and check out the dogs' expressions.

Answer:
The black lab mix in the center of page 148 is the least stressed dog in this photo series, but even this dog would be more comfortable without being restrained. Did you say the yellow lab to the right? His body language shows he's trying to move away from the boy.

Not Exactly Hallmark Moments . . .

This stressful series of photos shows the same boy and dog over a period of 2 years. Each one makes me uncomfortable for a different reason. The yorkie signals beautifully, but clearly no one is reading her body language.

#1. It's always best to have an adult in photos with an infant and a dog.

#2. Notice the dog's stiff body language and half-moon eyes. She wants more space, but the boy is coming right toward her. Most dog bites to children are on the face.

#3. The dog is eyeing the boy's cookie. Will she snatch it?

#4. The boy is squishing the dog. She clearly wants to get away. Notice her arched back and how she's looking directly into the boy's face.

#5. The boy is offering a treat, but the dog is still busy eating the first one. (She's turned away and is showing half-moon eye.) This could result in a resource-guarding issue.

Where's Sheba's Nose?

"Show me Sheba's nose. Very good! Now show me Sheba's ear." That's what I hear in my mind when I look at this photo. The little girl is gently, with a single finger, touching the dog's nose.

The dog is showing tolerance, not enjoyment.
Teach your children to identify your body parts, not your dog's.

Stop That Photo Op!

In general, dogs are very tolerant creatures. They' allow us to do many things that they don't enjoy. But that doesn't make it right.

Dogs are not horses.

Children should not be allowed to sit or lie on any dog. While the desire to do so is natural, it's not safe and it's not fair.

A parent should never, ever, place a child upon the dog's back as shown in the dalmatian photo.

No photo op is worth damaging the relationship between your child and your dog.

Be smart about how you set things up.

Stop That Photo Op!

"Stay!" When I look at this German shepherd, I'm very aware that the dog has been told to stay. His body language and attention are clearly focused on someone out of view rather than on the child slipping off his back.

Notice the front paws of the golden as she moves away from the girl lying on her side.

The labrador at left looks morose; he's not sharing the girl's sunny smile.

And this little pug has had enough. His early warning signals were missed.

This bite was preventable. Don't let it happen to your child.

Is This a Happy Face?

Pay particular attention to stress signals when setting up posed photos of your kids and dog. (See pages 36-37 for more info.)

Say Hi to the Nice Doggy!

The body language shown by these three dogs is very stiff and unwelcoming.

Just looking at these photos makes me hold my breath! It is not a good time to pet any of them.

It's much better to stand several feet away and invite the dog to approach you. (A full description of the three steps for meeting a dog can be found on pages 111-113.)

Giving Space

Though our faces and bodies are different, dogs and people have very similar body language. Whenever you are wondering how a dog is feeling, it can be beneficial to mimick the body language and ask yourself what emotional state the posture conveys.

The bulldog on the right is not comfortable with the white bulldog. He is is leaning away in an attempt to make a stressful moment easier.

Similarly the golden retriever in the second photo is leaning away from the child.

In the third photo, it's the little girl who is leaning away. The dog's body language shows discomfort as well.

That's Not Funny!

Many people like to tease dogs to provoke "funny" reactions. Most of these responses, however, are stress signals. For example, this young man is encouraging his dog to snarl at him. Teasing is a form of bullying and should be stopped at once.

Yours, Mine, or Ours?

Watch carefully when your dog is eating or chewing on something. Resource guarding is a common cause of dog bites to children.

We all guard our stuff to varying levels. Your toddler will fuss when another child takes her cookie. That's a form of resource guarding.

In a similar situation, your dog may simply feel sad about it...or she may bite. There's a huge range of responses, and the level of intensity will be affected by the dog's stress level.

These photos do not show safe interactions. Carefully supervise your children whenever your dog has something that she particularly values.

Barriers

Don't allow your kids to pet dogs who are in crates or cars, behind fences, or tied up. Many dogs feel threatened in these situations and may behave more aggressively than they would under normal circumstances.

It's common to want to comfort these dogs by offering attention, but your child's good intentions could be misinterpreted...with dangerous results.

Don't do it.

It's All Fun and Games Until Someone Gets Hurt

Every parent can recognize the moment when play starts to get out of control. As the energy level rises, so do the risks. Early intervention can help bring things down a notch and keep everyone safe and happy.

When kids get too revved up, they often push, shove, and grab.

Your dog doesn't have hands. When she wants to reach out and grab someone, she'll do it with her mouth. This can be both scary and dangerous.

The dog in the center photo is too spun up and needs a chance to settle down. Taking frequent breaks is an important part of managing play.

The puppy in the bottom photo is in over his head. His body language very stressed. This is a pretty extreme reaction for such a young dog.

By supervising carefully and intervening often, you can help prevent your dog from finding herself in an enough-already situaton. Knowing that she can rely on you for help will teach your dog that she doesn't have to handle stressful situations on her own.

Best Friends

Lest you think I'm just a grouch who finds fault with everything, here are a few photos that make me smile.

They're not perfect, but they demonstrate the love and companionship that great kid-and-dog relationships provide.

Enjoy!

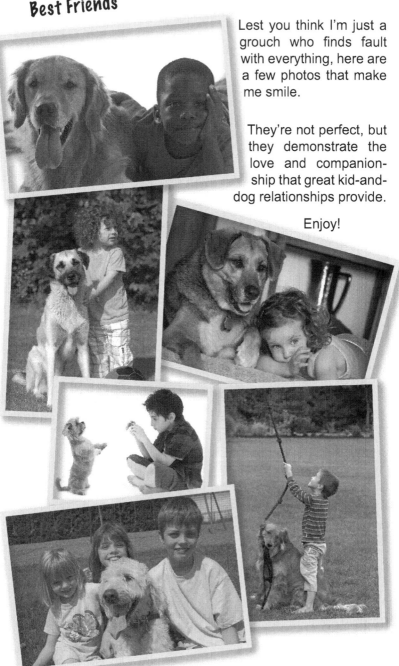

This photo my sons Kyle and Brandon with Gordo was used on the cover of the first edition of *Living with Kids and Dogs* back in 2005. My, how time flies.

Recommended Resources

Finding a Good Trainer

Ask a lot of question of any trainer you consider hiring. Be sure that you choose only trainers who use gentle, humane methods that do not rely on force, fear, or physical manipulation and make sure your trainer loves working with kids too!

Association of Pet Dog Trainers (APDT), 1-800-PET-DOGS, www.apdt.com. APDT supports and encourages continuing education for dog trainers. Search by region to find a trainer in your area.

Certification Council for Professional Dog Trainers (CCPDT), 212-356-0682, www.ccpdt.org. Trainers with a CPDT designation have passed a nationally administered qualifications exam.

International Association of Animal Behavior Consultants (IAABC), www.iaabc.org. Certified Dog Behavior Consultants evaluate, manage, and modify a wide range of challenging canine behaviors. They build and strengthen relationships between the human and canine members of a household.

Books and Periodicals

Before and After You Get Your Puppy, Ian Dunbar. The information contained in these books (they are published both separately and together) is what every trainer would like to tell families before they get a dog. *Before . . .* is available as a free download from www.siriuspup.com.

Click for Joy, Melissa Alexander (Sunshine, 2003). This book, written in Q&A format, is a great introduction to clicker training.

For the Love of a Dog, Patricia McConnell (Ballantine, 2006). A fascinating look at emotions in dogs. I think the fear chapter should be required reading for everyone who has a reactive dog.

Help for Your Fearful Dog, Nicole Wilde (Phantom, 2006). It's sad to have a dog who worries all the time. This book is full of hope and practical suggestions for helping your dog to become more confident.

Housetraining For Dummies, Susan McCullough (Wiley, 2002). Any number of variables can complicate house-training. This book covers them in detail.

How to Teach a New Dog Old Tricks, Ian Dunbar (James & Kenneth, 1996). Packed with information stated so clearly, you'll smack your forehead and say, "Why didn't I think of that?"

Mine: A Practical Guide to Resource Guarding in Dogs, Jean Donaldson (Kinship Communications, 2002). Resource guarding is a very serious problem. This book outlines a labor-intensive, scientifically sound behavior modification program.

Playtime for Your Dog, Christina Sondermann (Cadmos, 2006). A superb book filled with simple and complex activities for you and your dog. No matter what age your children are, you'll find something fun for them to do with your dog.

The Power of Positive Dog Training, Pat Miller (Howell, 2001). This book, by the training editor of Whole Dog Journal, is full of good training tips and lots of things your teen (or dog-crazy elementary schooler) may enjoy.

Puppy Training for Kids, Colleen Pelar (Barrons, 2012). Written for kids between 8 and 12, this book has lots of information about training, body language, and behavior. I focused on puppies, but much of the content applies equally well to adult dogs.

Senior Dogs For Dummies, Susan McCullough (Wiley, 2004). We all have special needs as we age. Dogs are no different. Learn how to help your dog with the challenges of aging.

Toolbox for Remodeling Your Problem Dog, Terry Ryan (Dogwise, 2010). Terry Ryan is a creative problem solver and committed to positive training methods. Her books are filled practical and innovative ideas.

Whole Dog Journal. Simply the best periodical out there. Probably more in-depth than most pet owners really want, but if you are a true dog nut, add this to your birthday wish list. You'll be glad you did. www.whole-dog-journal.com

Videos

Clicker Puppy, Doggone Crazy. This 48-minute video shows children safely training and playing with puppies. Watch it to learn fun training activities you and your kids can do with your puppy. www.clickertraining.com

Language of Dogs, Sarah Kalnajs. Fascinated by canine body language? Then this 133-minute DVD set is for you! (It's more than the casual viewer will want.) There's a huge variety of body types among dogs, so I love that this program shows several different dogs doing each of the signals. You'll be much better at reading dogs after watching this program.

New Puppy! Now What? Victoria Schade. In this award-winning video's 38 fun-filled minutes, you'll get lots of easy-to-implement tips for getting off to a great start with your new puppy. Closed captioned.

Take a Bow . . . Wow!; Bow Wow, Take 2; and **The How of Bow Wow,** Virginia Broitman and Sherri Lippman. These trick-training videos are fun to watch and full of good tips on how to train behaviors. www.takeabowwow.com

Websites Worth Visiting

Doggone Crazy game, www.doggonecrazy.com. This fun family board game features stacks of cards, and you and your kids must answer whether it is safe to interact with the dog shown. The answer and explanation are included on the back of each card. Great for trainers to use in schools as well.

Doggone Safe, www.doggonesafe.com. Doggone Safe is a non-profit organization dedicated to dog bite prevention education for children, families, and workers and dog bite victim support.

Family Paws Parent Education, www.familypaws.com. This site has Jennifer Shryock's highly regarded parent programs: Dogs & Storks for the infant stage and the Dog & Baby Connection program for families with young kids. (Cat information coming soon!). Check the directory to find a presenter near you.

Living with Kids and Dogs, www.livingwithkidsanddogs.com. This is my site, and I have a lot of information about helping kids be safe around dogs. Check out the videos of dogs being hugged, kissed, and patted on the head.

Index

About Colleen Pelar

For more than 20 years of helping parents navigate the challenges of living with kids and dogs, Colleen Pelar has honed a unique perspective filled with humor and practical, easy-to-implement tips for success. Colleen wants to ensure that kids and dogs have happy, healthy relationships.

To further that goal, she has written three books, *Living with Kids and Dogs . . . Without Losing Your Mind*, *Kids and Dogs: A Professional's Guide to Helping Families* and *Puppy Training for Kids.*

In addition to teaching classes and seeing clients at All About Dogs in northern Virginia, Colleen gives presentations around the country, educating people about how to live safely with kids and dogs. She has also served as an instructor at the Washington D.C. Metropolitan Police Academy where she taught police officers how to interact with the many dogs they encounter on the job.

An active member of the Association of Pet Dog Trainers (APDT) and the International Association of Animal Behavior Consultants (IAABC), Colleen regularly attends dog-training seminars and has earned the Certified Professional Dog Trainer (CPDT-KA) and Certified Dog Behavior Consultant (CDBC) titles.